DRAWING MADE EASY

BY

JOSEPH CUMMINGS CHASE

Author of " Decorative Design "

Supervisor Art Department, Townsend Harris Hall
College of the City of New York

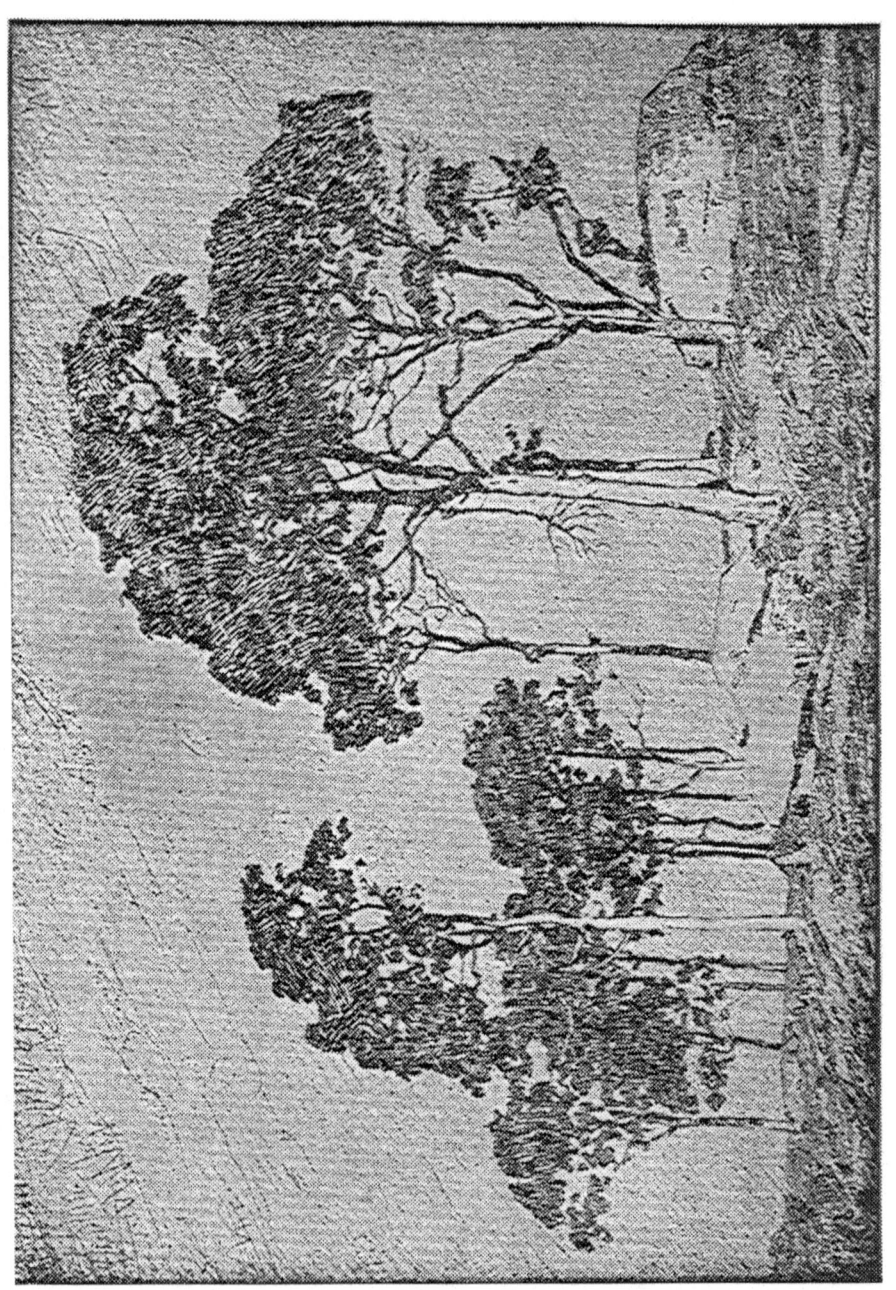

Drawing in ink and pencil by A. G. Schulman.
See chapter on Pictorial Composition, p. 91.

DRAWING MADE EASY

Drawing Made Easy

THE *accuracy* of drawing is a matter of mathematics — ratio and proportion. The ability to draw accurately can be cultivated to a surprising degree by the average student, young or old. It is easy to understand that two drawings made by two different students may be practically equal as to accuracy while one may have beauty and the other may not. So the process of accurate drawing is not *art;* a drawing may or may not possess art expression. Drawing may be likened to a tool which the artist should possess, just as an efficient carpenter should possess a hammer, in order to facilitate his efforts. Further, it can be understood that many an excellent draughtsman is not an artist at all, in the exact sense, and many an artist is not a good draughtsman, and, thus lacking a very necessary tool, is forever handicapped in his efforts to express his conception upon paper or upon canvas.

(*a*) In order that his drawings may be accurate, the draughtsman must understand the simple rules of perspective and must know how to measure the relative proportions of whatever objects may confront him.

(*b*) In order that his drawings may be treated with an effect of beauty, the draughtsman must further understand something of "treatment" and the basic principles of design (which includes "composition"). An understanding of the simple rules of perspective and of the principles of design is by no means difficult for the average mind. An understanding of "treatment," however, is not always so easy to acquire.

Now as to *perspective:* The reader will find the following paragraphs perfectly simple if he will refer to the diagrams and drawings on pages 14, 17, 19, 24, 25, and 26.

There is nothing alarming about " simple perspective " except the name.

In perspective we draw an object not as it really is, but as it appears to be. This is not hard to understand, surely. We know that a cube has six faces and that each of them is a square and that all of these six squares are of equal length and breadth. But we do not draw the cube thus for the simple reason that it does not so appear as we look at the cube. We may see three faces of the cube (if it is opaque), or two, or only one. If it is a glass cube we may be able to see all six of its faces, but even then those faces will appear to be varied as to shape and measurements. An object near at hand appears to be larger than the same object further away. Thus the face of the cube which is nearest the onlooker appears larger than the face further away. This matter of appearance is what we need to

PERSPECTIVE OF THE CUBE

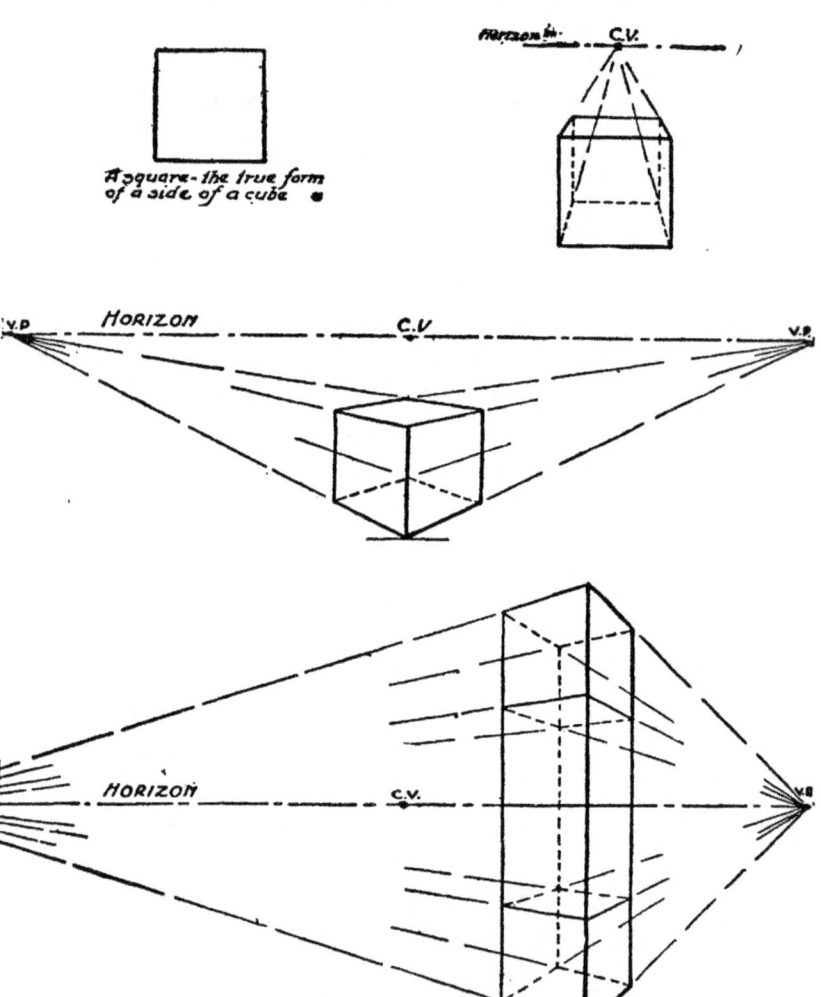

A square-the true form of a side of a cube

The cube at top, right, is in " parallel" perspective. Four of its horizontal edges have only one vanishing point, which in this case is at the same point as the center of vision.

The other cubes are in " angular" perspective having two vanishing points for their horizontal edges.

The four cubes in the bottom figure have only two vanishing points, because all their edges are parallel to each other.

comprehend about perspective, but to reproduce accurately on paper the appearance of an object in perspective requires certain helps.

The only object which is an exception, in that its appearance of form does not vary with every change of position, is a sphere.

We observe that the horizontal edges of objects seem to be tending upwards (if below the eye) or downwards (if above the eye) or sideways, as the case may be, although actually we know that these edges are perfectly level and horizontal. We also observe that lines and objects that we know to be parallel seem to approach each other and diminish in size as their distance from the onlooker increases; likewise circular surfaces appear as ellipses, from certain points of view becoming so narrow that they appear only as straight lines. If we look along a straight street we notice that the upper lines of the buildings appear to be descending as the distance increases, and their lower lines ascending, these upper and lower horizontal lines all tending to a point on the horizon. The checker-board illustrated on page 17 shows very clearly this appearance of convergence. As a result of observing these appearances, which we know to be different from the actualities, we arrive at certain basic statements of facts concerning perspective.

In perspective all parallel horizontal lines seem to converge toward a point on the horizon called a " vanishing point." See the middle of page 14 and notice that this cube shows two sets of parallel horizontal lines and therefore has two vanishing points on the horizon. When a second cube *B* is placed, corner on corner, upon the first cube *A* (see bottom of page 14) its two sets of parallel horizontal lines have the same two vanishing points upon the same horizon as has the first cube *A*.

Now let us come to an understanding as to that much abused word " horizon."

PERSPECTIVE OF A CHECKER-BOARD

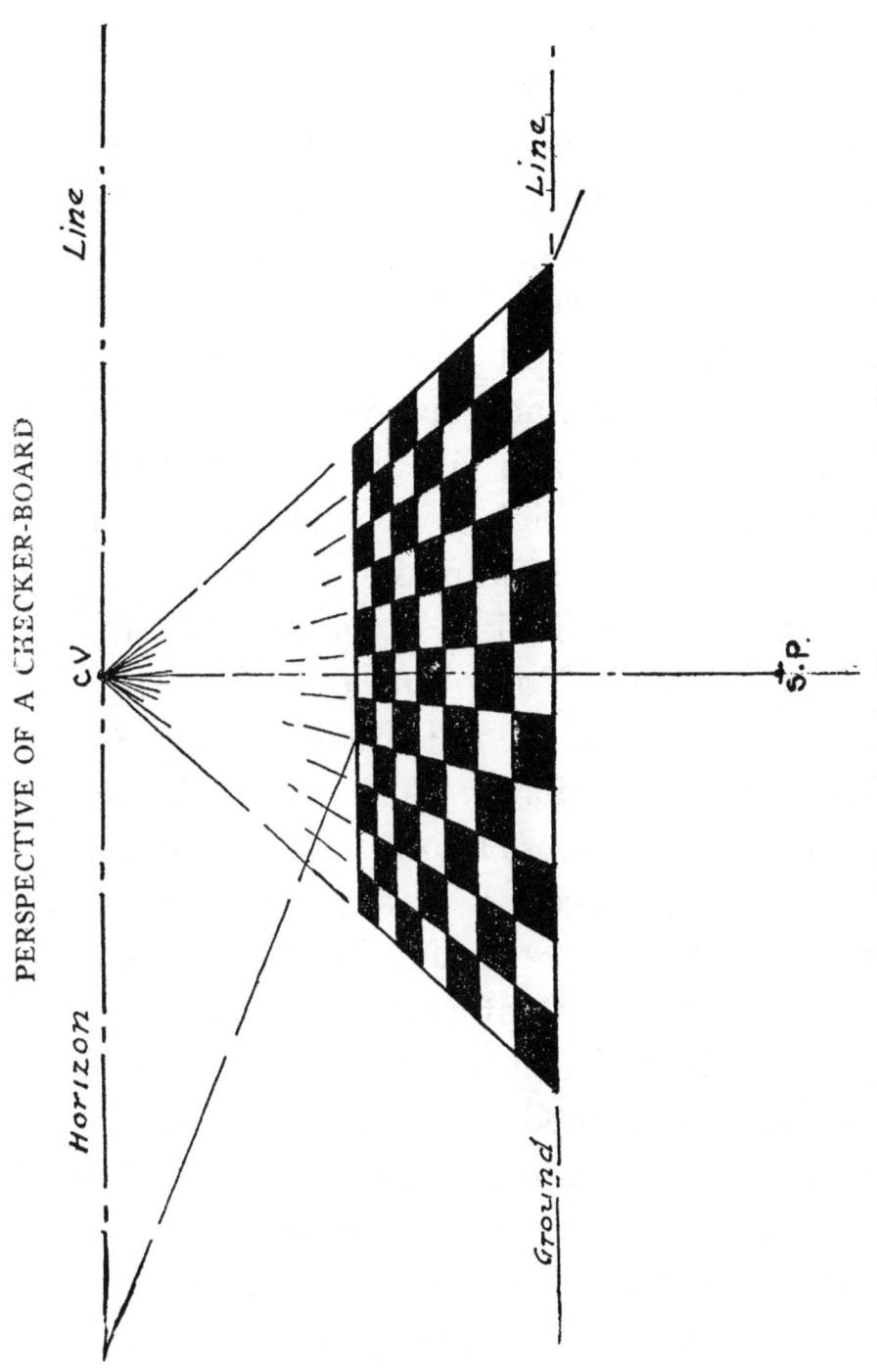

CV = center of vision, which in this case is the vanishing point.

Contrary to many a time-worn geography, the horizon *is not* " where the earth and sky seem to meet." If it were, how many a bent and twisted, up-hill and down-dale horizon there would be. You yourself have an horizon and you cannot escape it. Like taxes, it cannot be avoided. Moreover, your horizon is your individual property from which you cannot be separated except by blindness. It is not imaginary. It is real. It is *height,* and height is real. Your five feet and eight inches of height is not imaginary. Remember then, that *the horizon is the height of the onlooker's eye. Your* horizon is a plane surface, so to speak, extending away from you at the height of your eye as far as the sight of your eye can reach. Every object that you can see, so far as you are concerned, is either wholly or partly above or below *your* horizon. This horizon of yours becomes at once a wonderful assistance to you in drawing any and all objects, because you can reckon

HORIZON

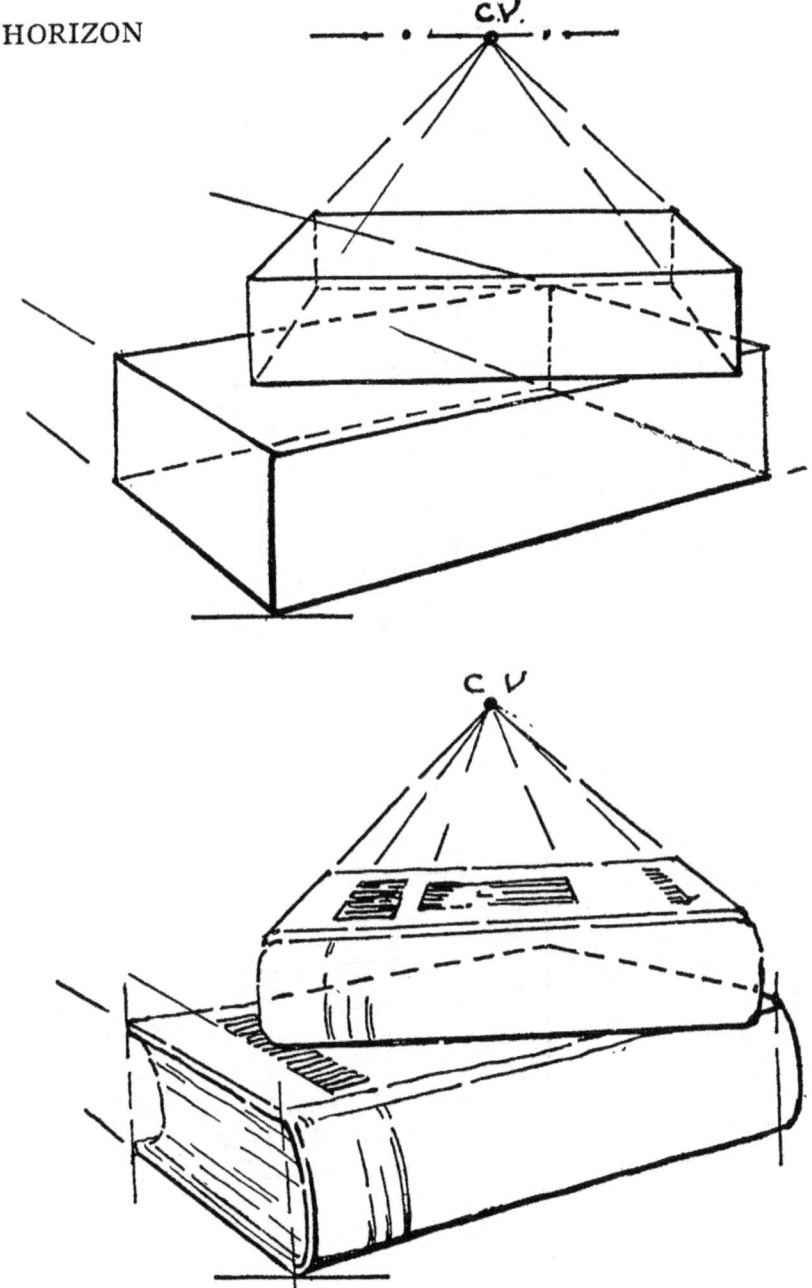

CV = *center of vision (on the horizon).*
The top book is in horizontal perspective.
The bottom book is in angular perspective.

PERSPECTIVE OF THE PRISM

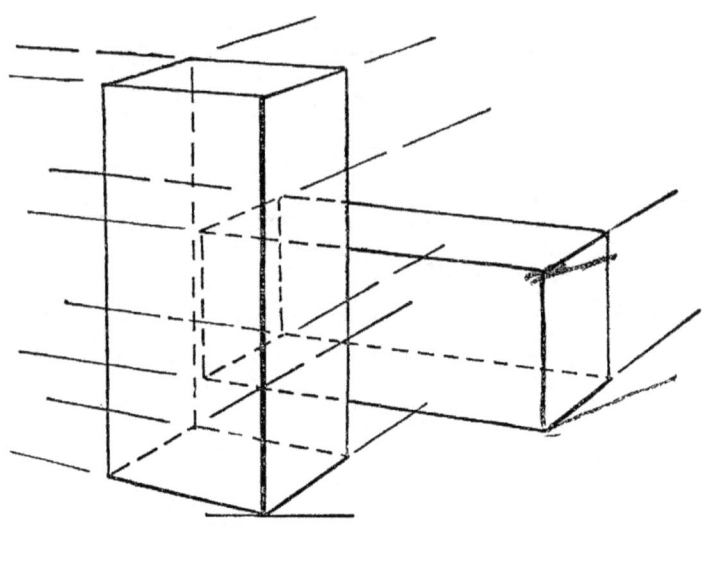

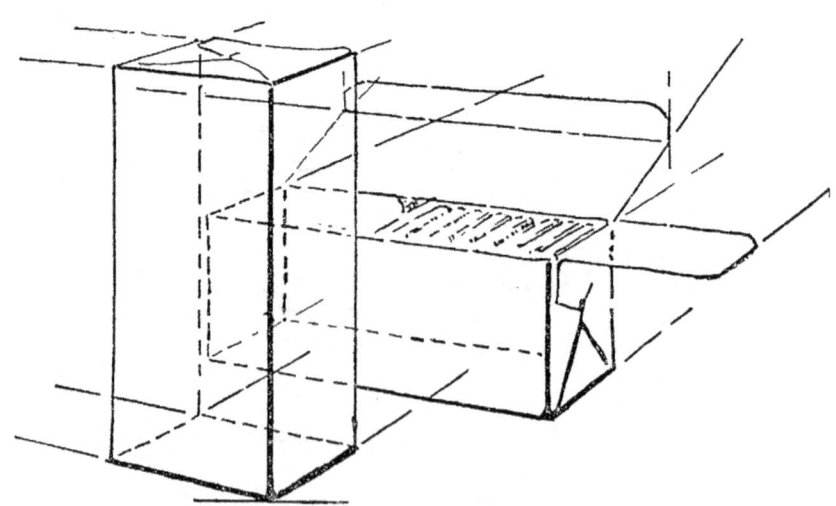

These drawings indicate why the beginner is directed to learn the construction of " blocks."

PERSPECTIVE OF SEVERAL SOLIDS

PERSPECTIVE OF SEVERAL SOLIDS

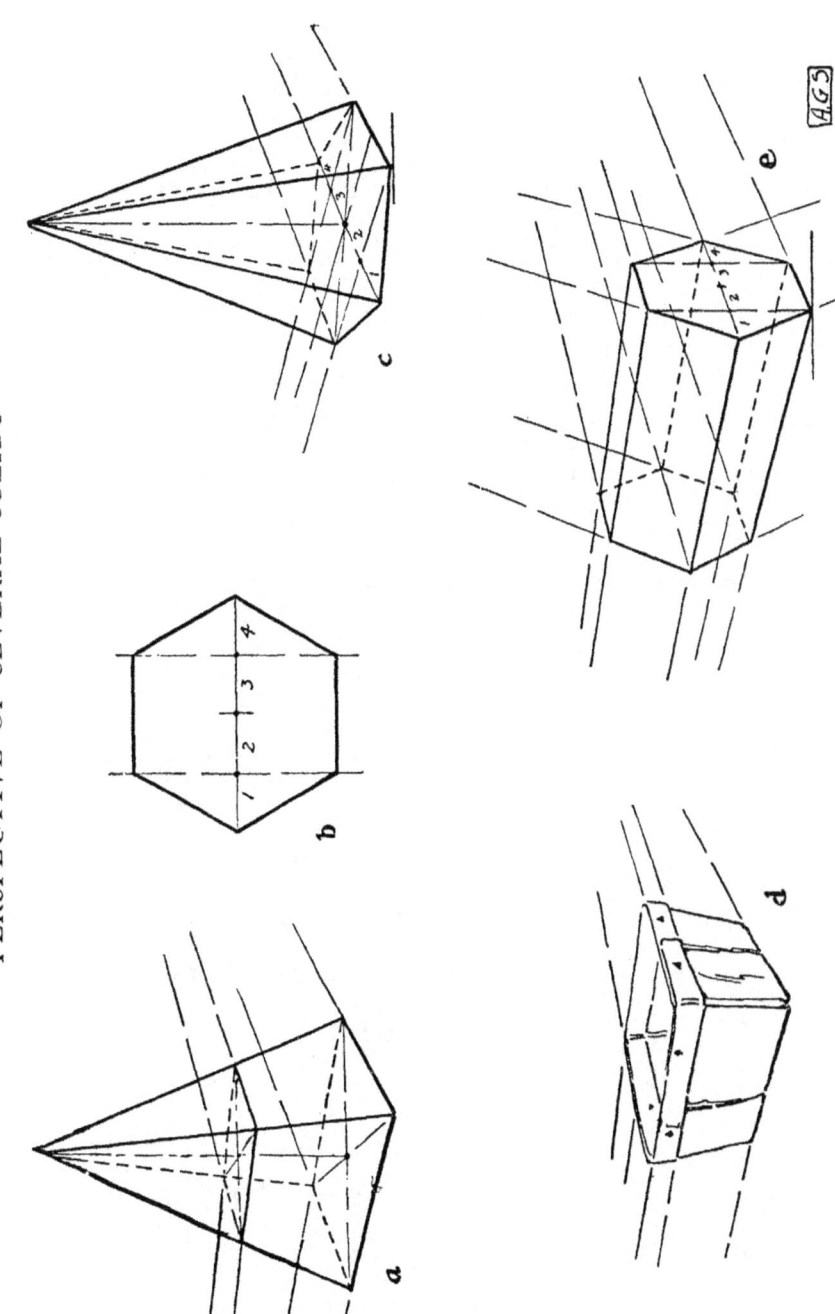

b *is a hexagon. Its long diagonal is divided into four equal parts. However, when seen in perspective, as in figures c and e, that part of the long diagonal marked 4 is slightly less than that marked 3. In like manner 3 is less than 2, and 2 is less than 1. Just because it is further away 4 appears to be less than 3.*

15

the proportionate distance of points above or below this horizon of yours. When you stand, your horizon is the height of your eye; seat yourself, and your horizon has become lowered to the new height of your eye. Walk into the house, up the stairs, look out of the second story window, if you please, and your horizon has ascended with you, and as you look out over the landscape, your horizon is still the height of your eye.

Before proceeding further let us agree upon the meaning of the word perpendicular.

The word *perpendicular* is not identical in meaning with the word vertical, for while a line to be vertical must be at right-angles (90 degrees) to the horizon, a straight line is perpendicular to any other straight line so long as it is at right-angles to it. Thus a horizontal line is as thoroughly perpendicular to a vertical line as is a vertical perpendicular to a horizontal, and any straight line at any slant

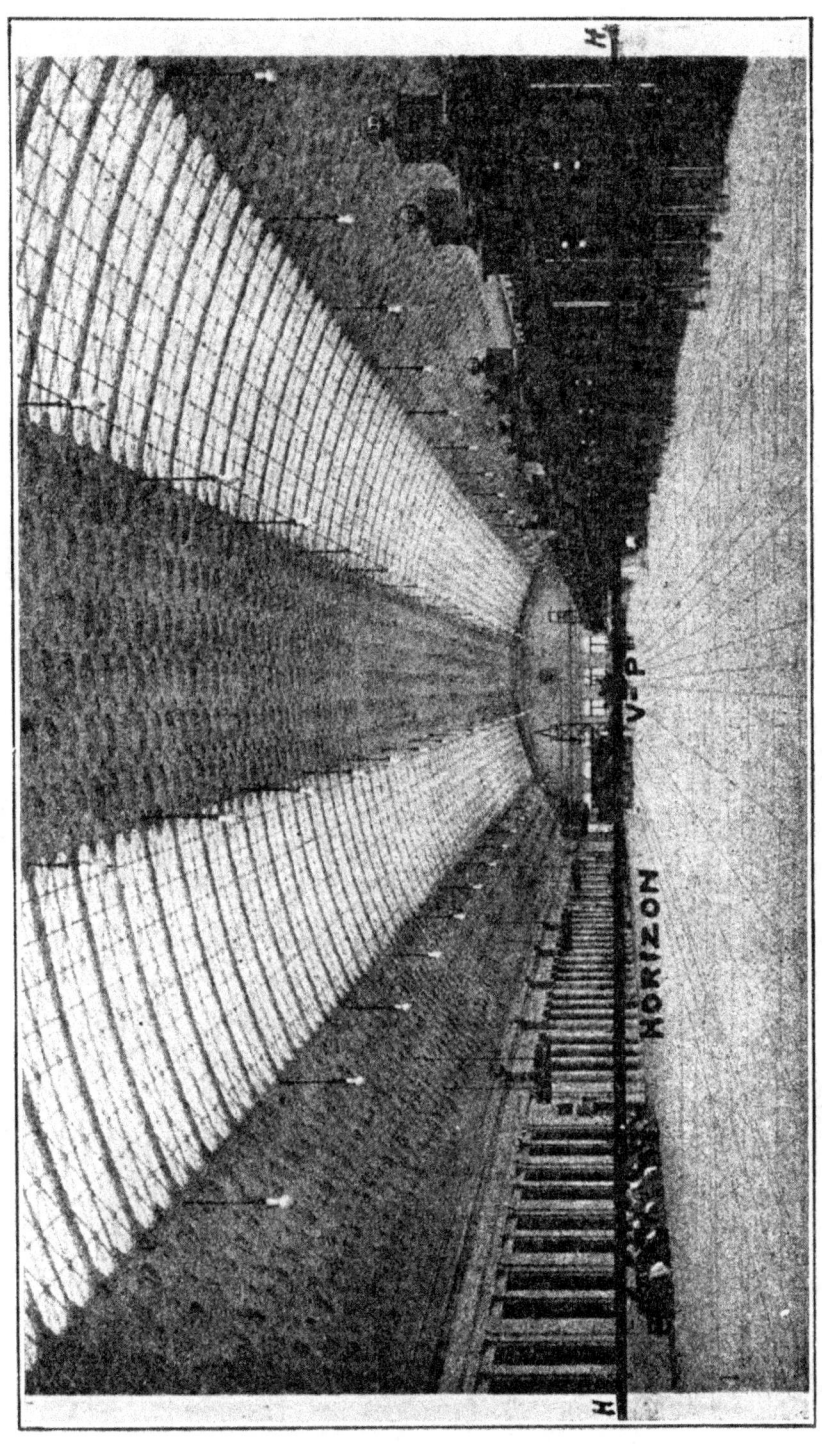

"All parallel horizontal lines seem to converge toward a point on the horizon called a vanishing point." The onlooker was standing on the main floor.

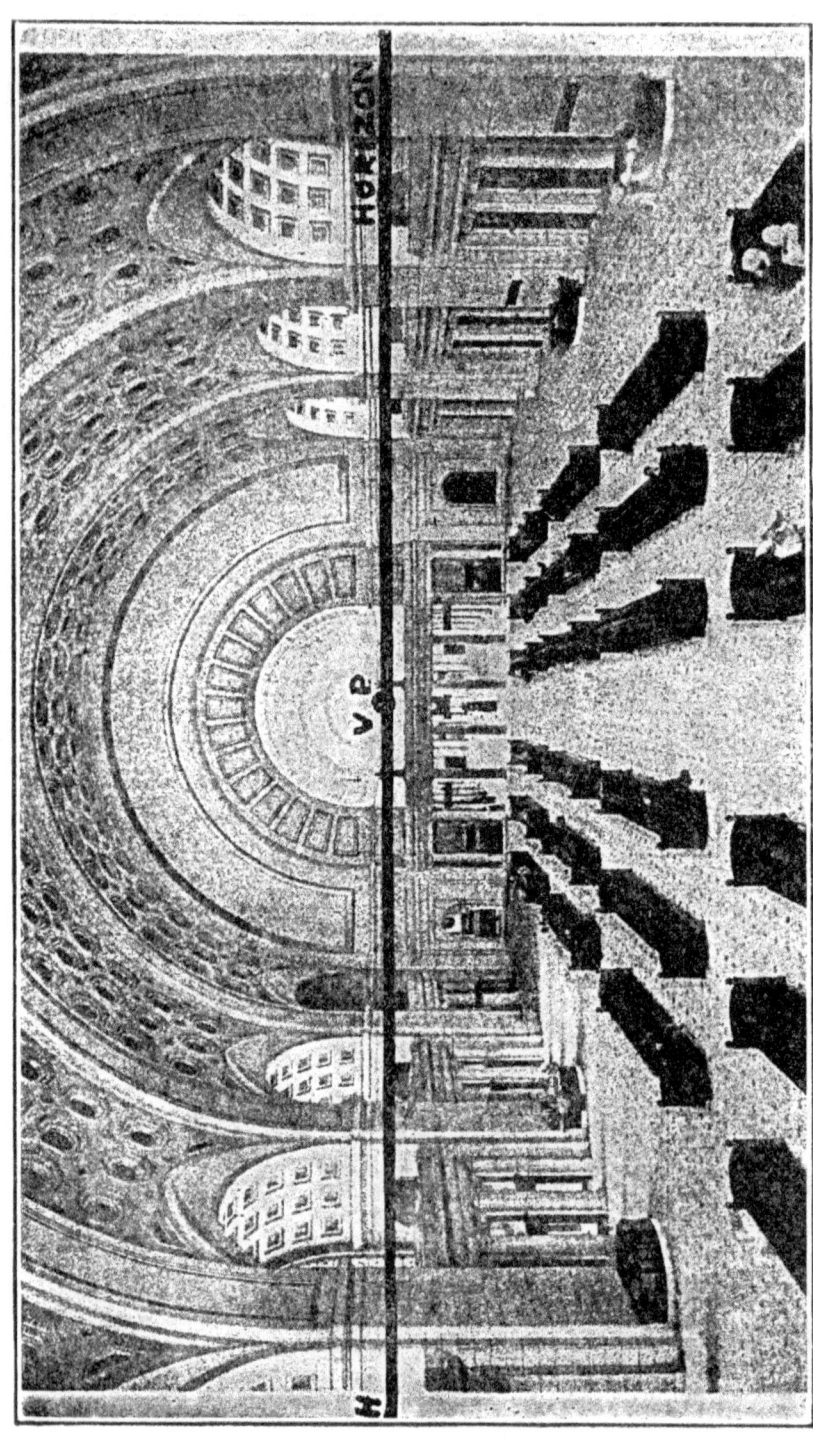

" All parallel horizontal lines seem to converge toward a point on the horizon called a vanishing point." The onlooker was standing in a gallery.

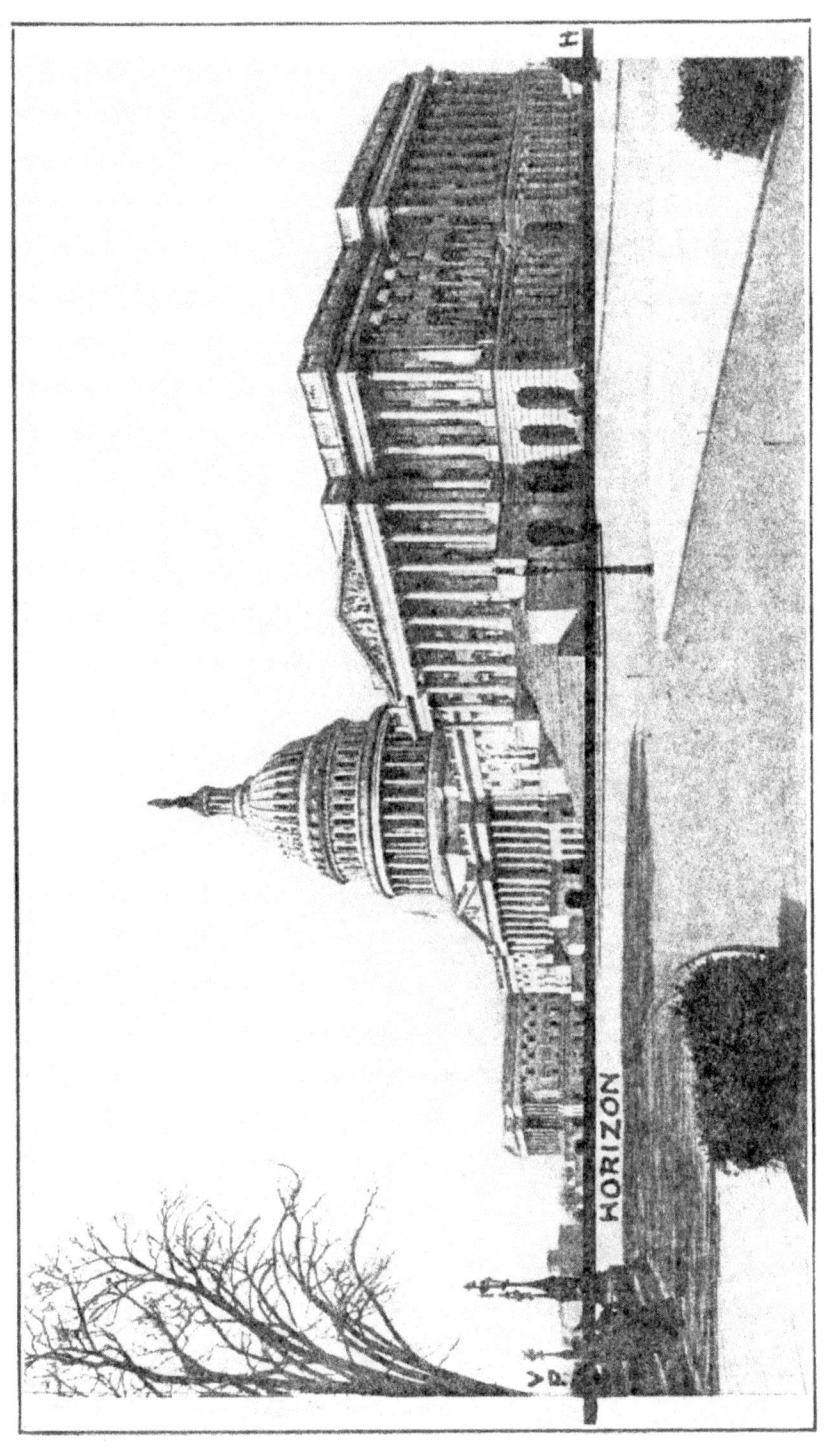

The two sets of parallel horizontal lines evident in the construction of this building are converging, each set toward a vanishing point. The one VP is at the left edge of the picture. The other VP is about one and three-quarter inches to the right of the picture. Both vanishing points are on the horizon.

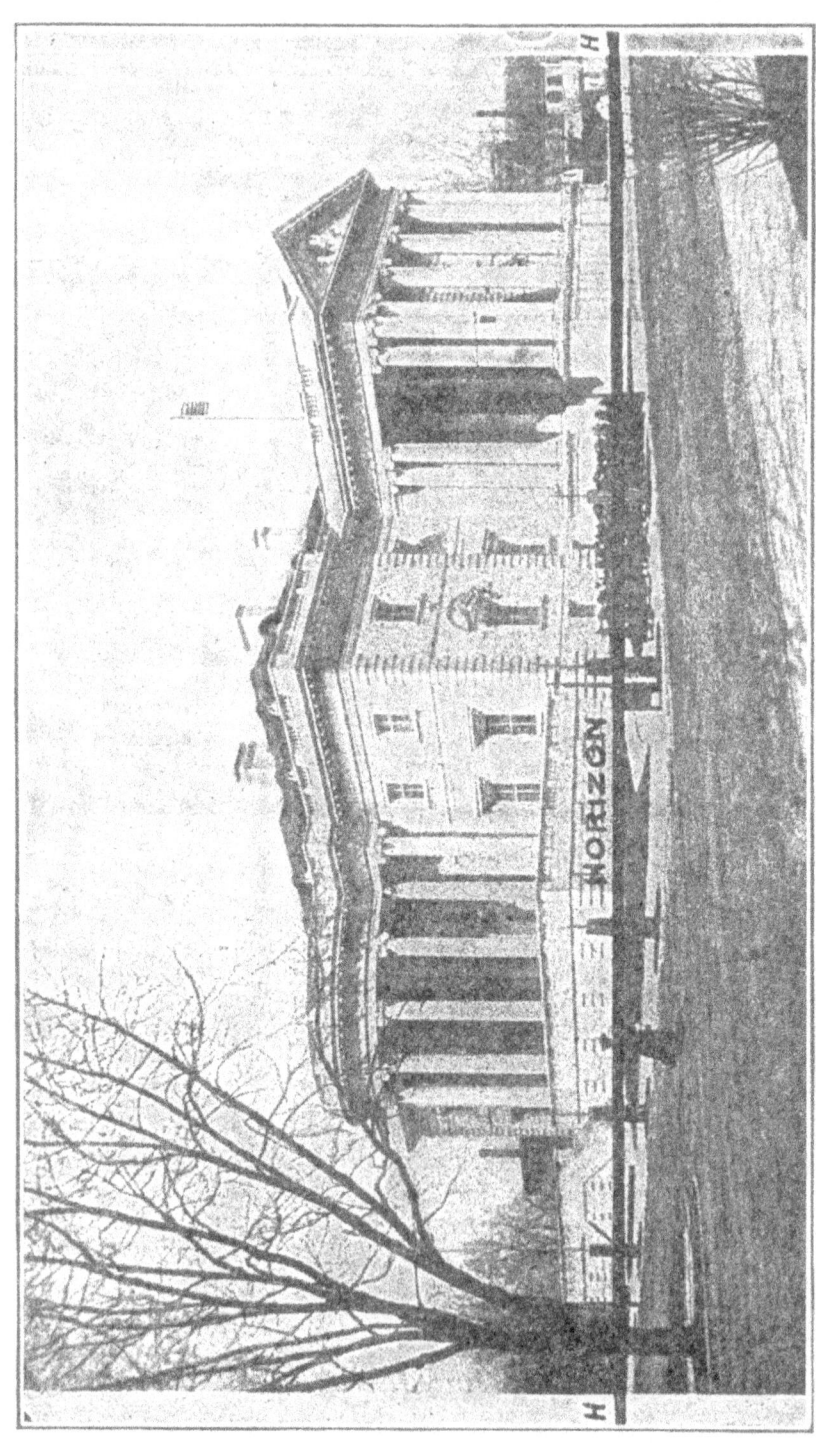

The two sets of parallel horizontal lines evident in the construction of this building are converging, each set toward a vanishing point. The one VP is about four inches to the left of the picture. The other VP is about two and one-half inches to the right of the picture. Both vanishing points are on the horizon.

is perpendicular to any other straight line which forms with it a right-angle (90 degrees). So perpendicular means " at right angles to."

If a camera photographs the Flatiron Building from a position near the base and is pointed upward toward the top of the building, it is evident that the photograph thus made will show the vertical lines of the building converging upward so that the top of the building will appear considerably smaller than the base. And yet, be it remembered that *in perspective all vertical lines are drawn vertical* and the draughtsman must draw the Flatiron Building not as the camera sees it, but with its vertical lines vertical, and not converging toward the top. (Notice that in the preceding sentence it was unnecessary to speak of all *parallel* vertical lines because all vertical lines *are* parallel.)

In drawing objects that have circular tops or bases, these tops or bases will ap-

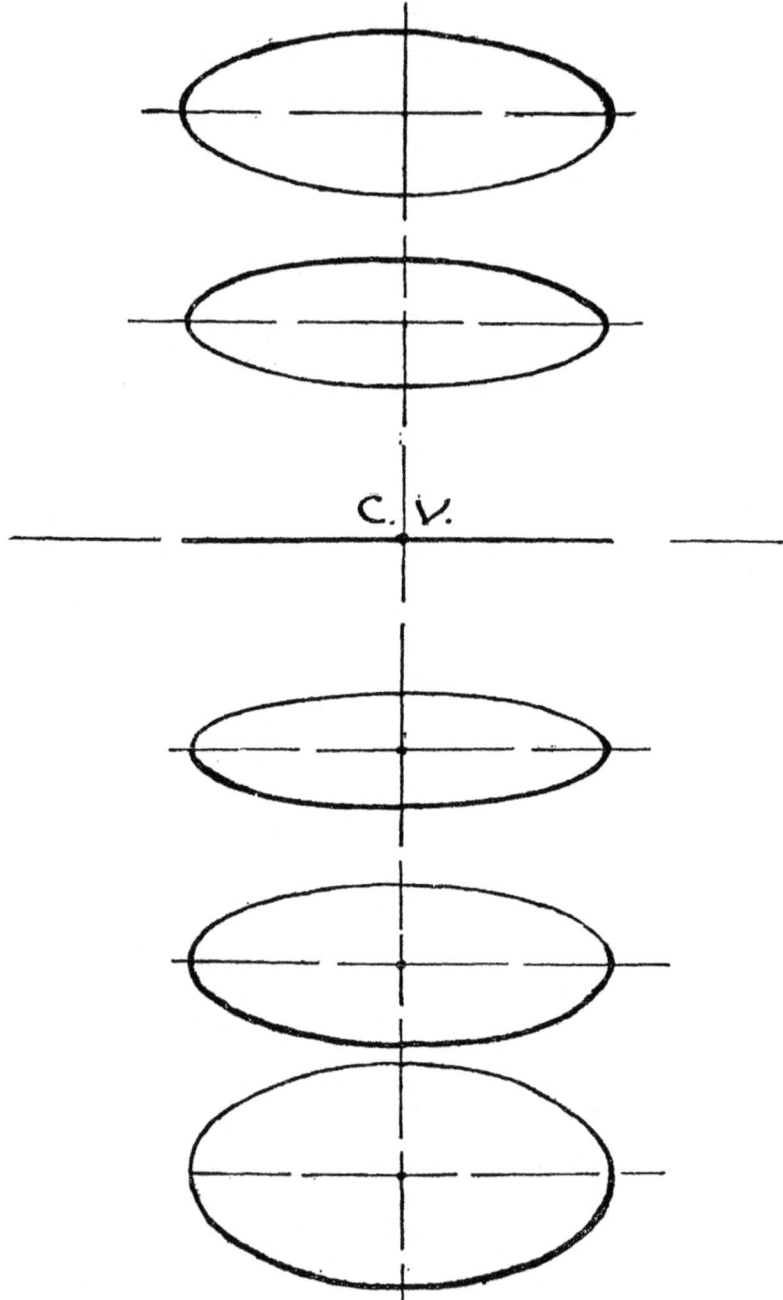

Two circles in perspective above the horizon, and three below the horizon.

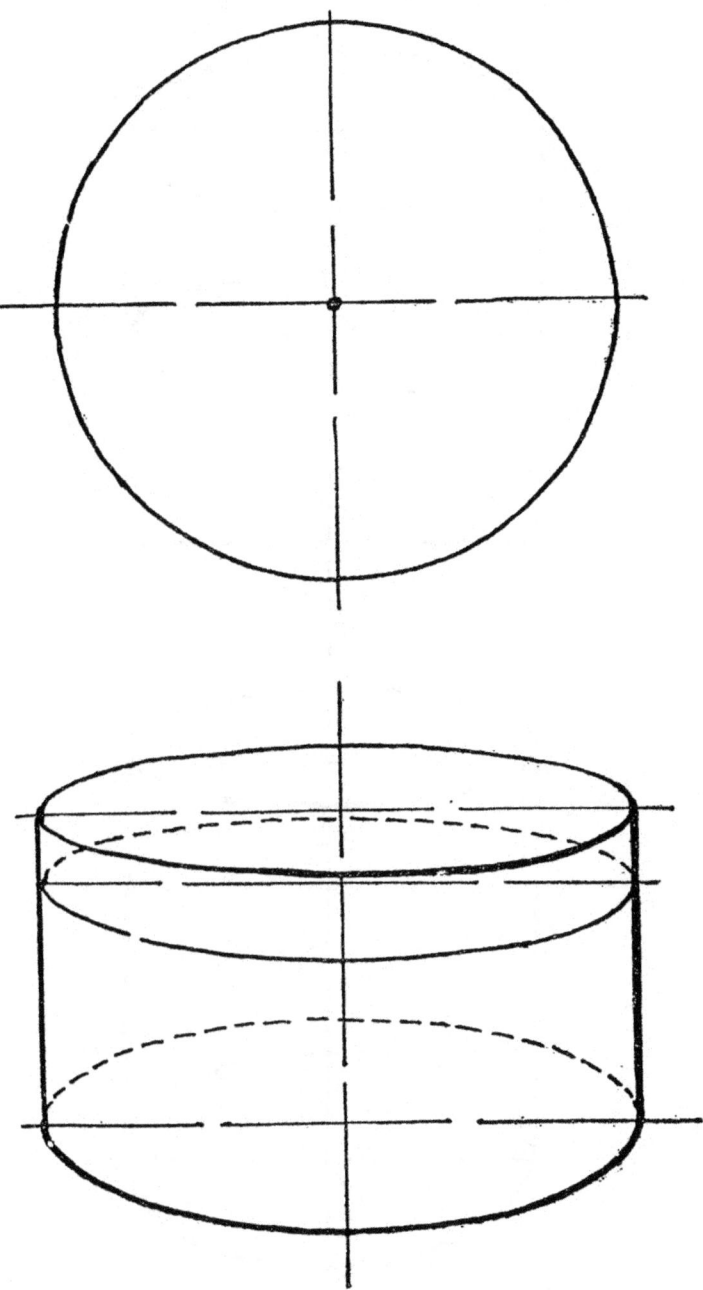

Above: *a circle.*
Below: *perspective of a hatbox, showing three circles in perspective (ellipses).*

PERSPECTIVE OF THE CIRCLE

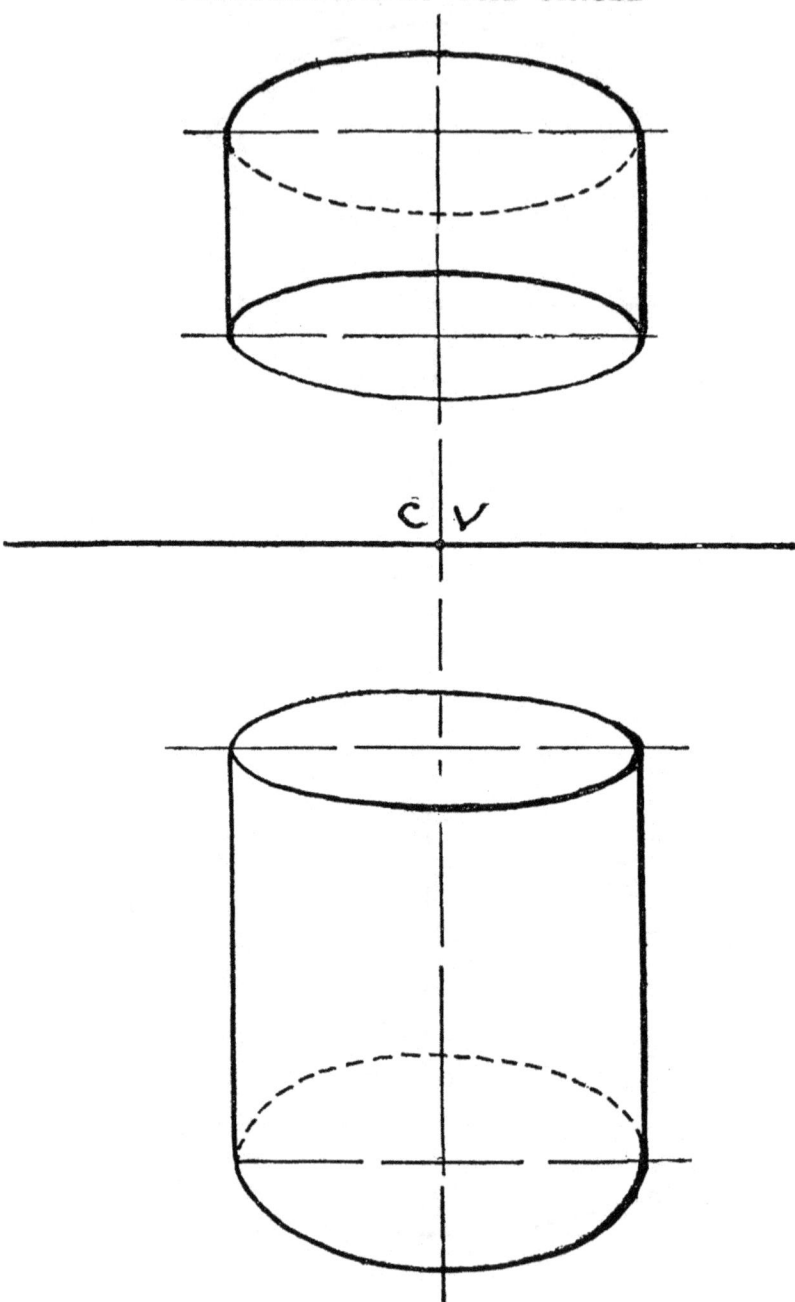

*One figure above the horizon, and
one below it.*

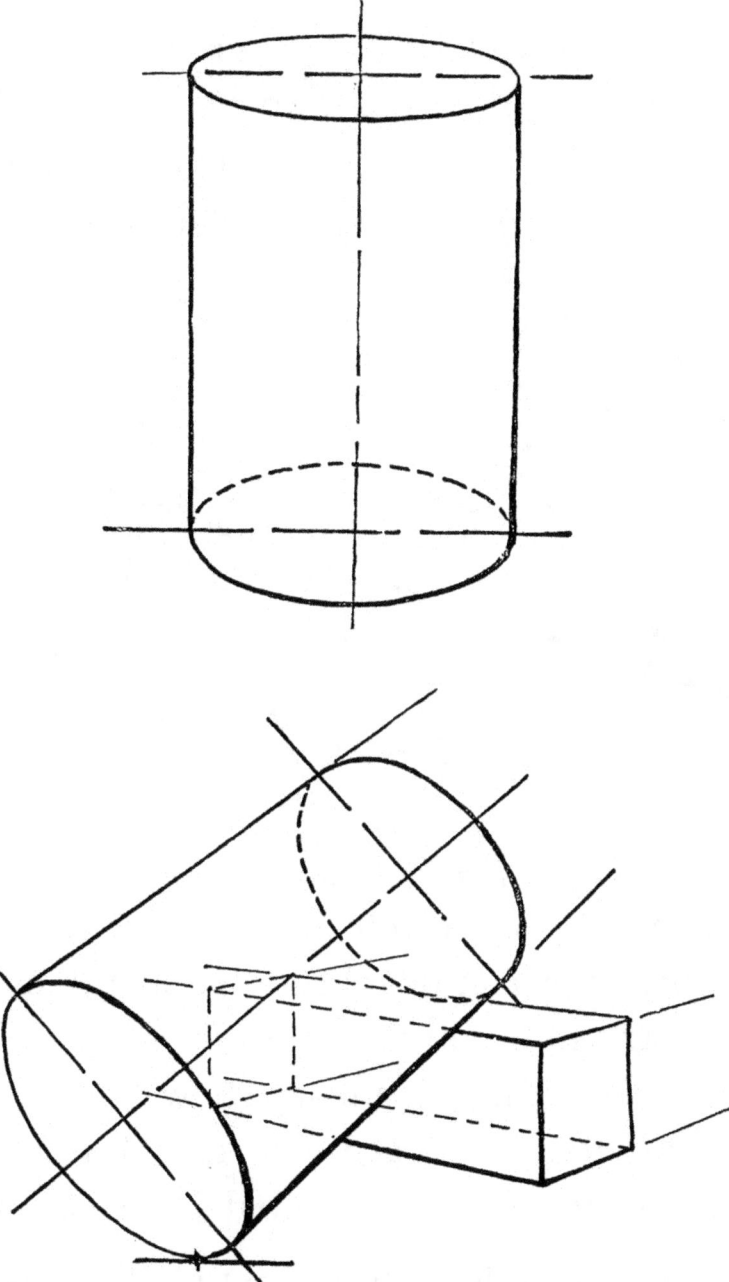

Notice in the lower figure that the long axis of the circles is perpendicular to the axis of the cylinder. Both figures below the horizon.

pear as ellipses.* The drawing of ellipses
is a matter which seems to be difficult for
beginners because of a failure to understand that an ellipse is shaped identically

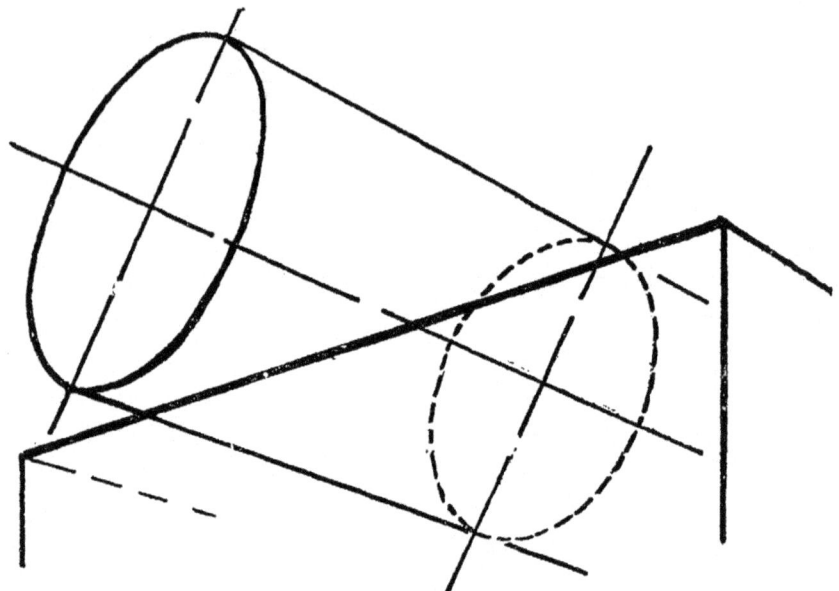

Perspective of the circle (above the horizon).

the same as is a circle in perspective, and
so being, *never* appears pointed at the ends,
no matter how narrow the ellipse may be.
If you, from the grandstand, were watch-
ing an automobile race on a circular track,
your position being such that the track ap-

NOTE A. A circle in perspective has the same contour as
an ellipse, but the middle line of the circle is farther back
than is the longest axis of the ellipse.

peared to be a narrow ellipse, the ends of
the ellipse would not appear pointed, and
as the automobiles tore around the ends of
the ellipse so circular would those ends

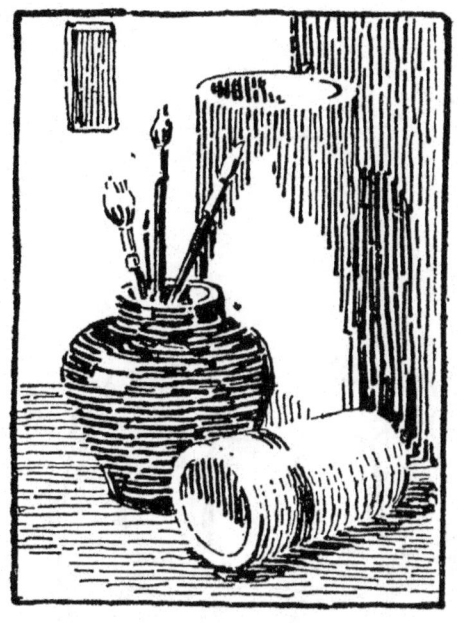

Perspective of the circle (above the horizon).

appear that you would never doubt the
ability of the motors to continue upon the
track. In drawing ellipses then, do not
make them so pointed at the ends that a
racing automobile could not make its way
safely around the ends. Those ends are
never like the small end of an egg—they

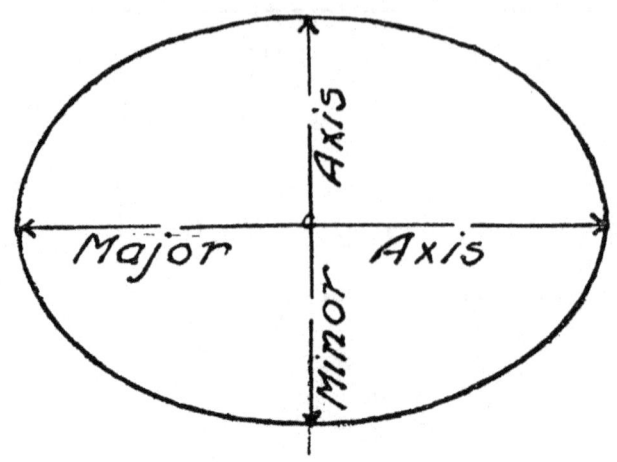

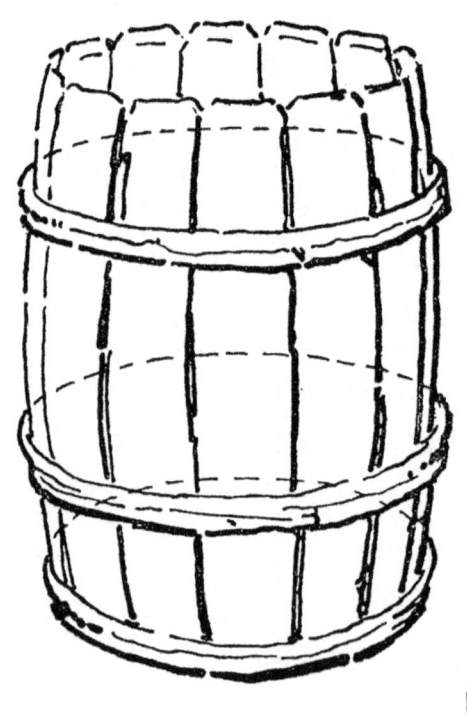

have much more the appearance of the big end of an egg.

A horizontally placed circle seen in perspective always has its longest axis horizontal. For example, if a horizontally placed table is seen in perspective with its parallel edges converging toward vanishing points upon the horizon, each dish upon the table has its longest axis horizontal and never appears to be slanting, as does the table top.

There are certain mathematical helps in drawing of which every student should avail himself. Some of these are illustrated on pages 14 and 49. For instance: If the base of an object is square,—as in a cube,—the side which appears to be narrower appears also to have its base line slanting at a sharper angle away from the horizontal, if the object is below the horizon. If above the horizon it is the top line instead of the base line which forms the sharper angle.

If a cube is placed below the horizon

PERSPECTIVE OF THE CIRCLE

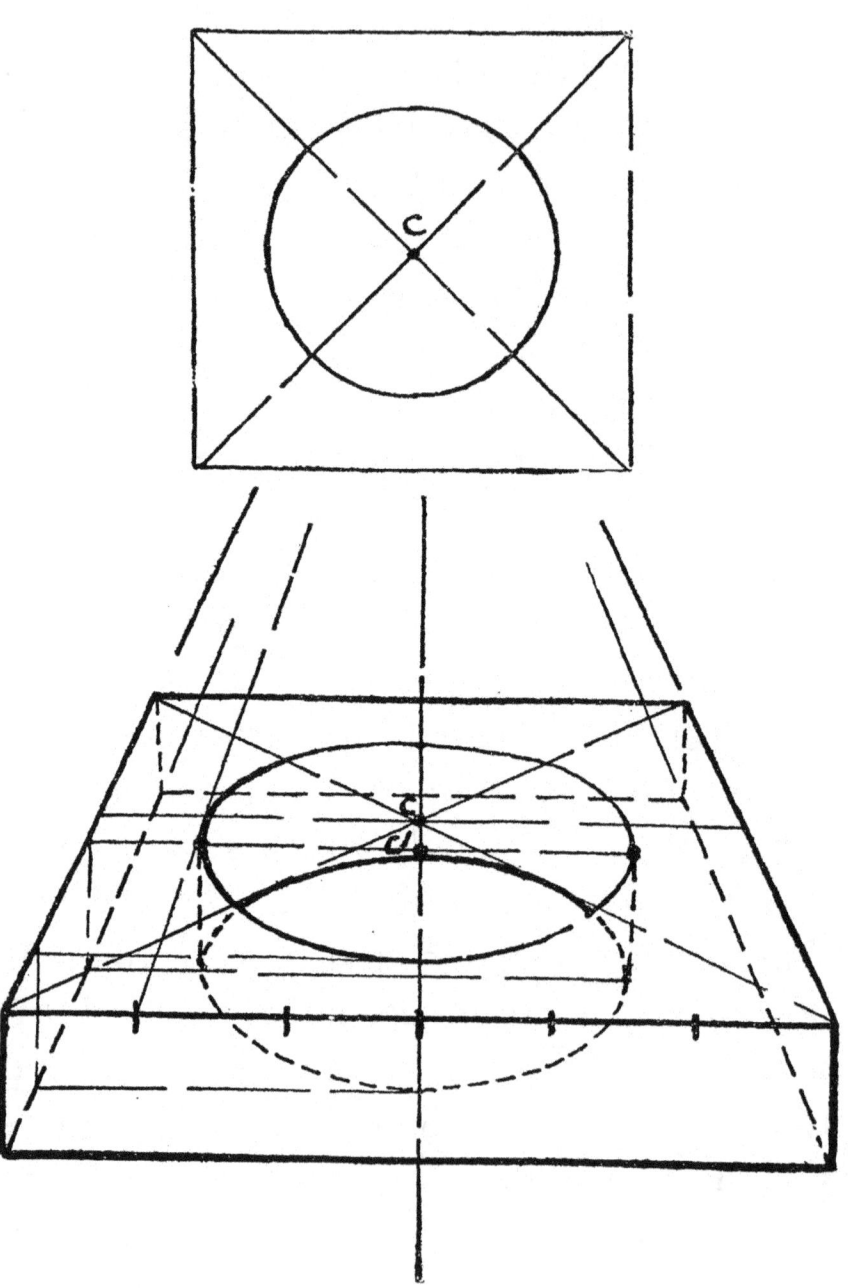

PERSPECTIVE OF THE CIRCLE

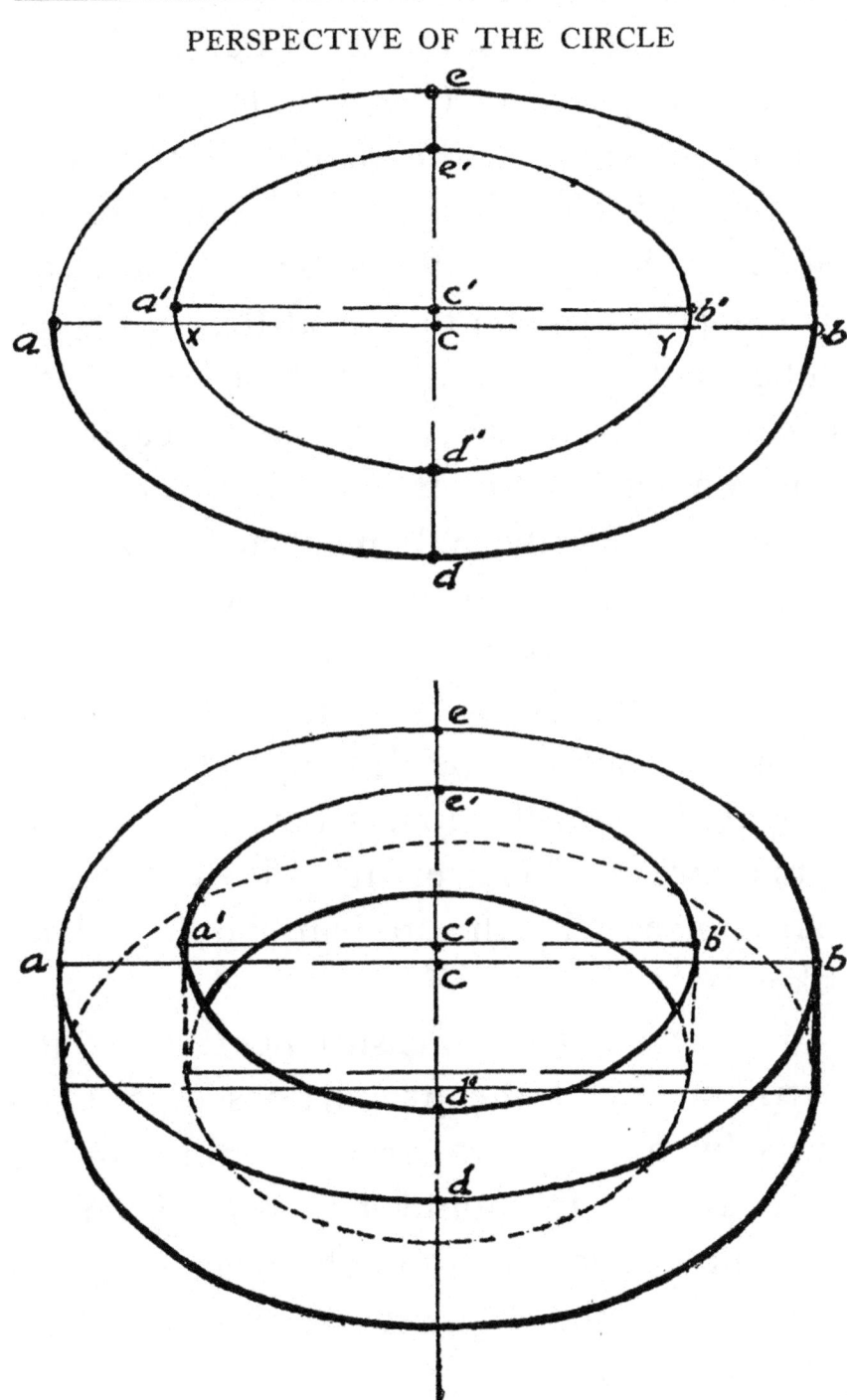

so that its top frontmost corner is distant from the horizon (the eye level) a distance the same as the height of the front vertical edge of the cube, the angle of the horizontal edges of the cube will be twice as sharp * at the bottom as at the top of the cube, and if the lines of these horizontal edges are continued until they reach the horizon, each set of the parallel horizontal edges of the cube will meet at a "vanishing point on the horizon." See page 14.

Some teachers of drawing are unwilling for their pupils to "measure" the dimensions of objects to be drawn, but since our most expert professionals never hesitate to "measure" whenever it will help, it is hard to see why the student should not do likewise.

However, any measurement that the artist makes of the proportions of the objects he proposes to draw is more or less inaccurate. It should be borne in mind that no matter how much measuring has been done, the unassisted eye is the final

* *Approximately.*

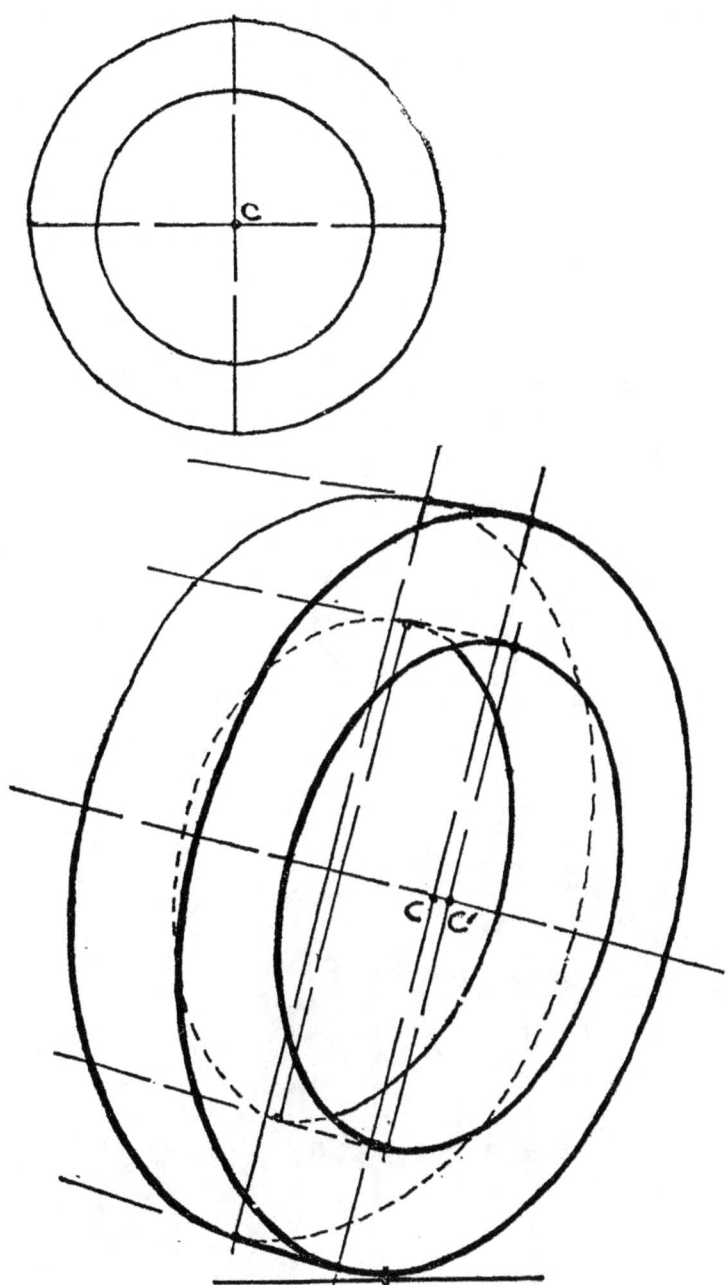

Notice that in the lower figure the long axis of each of the four ellipses is perpendicular to the center of the cylinder.

Drawing Made Easy

PERSPECTIVE OF THE CONE

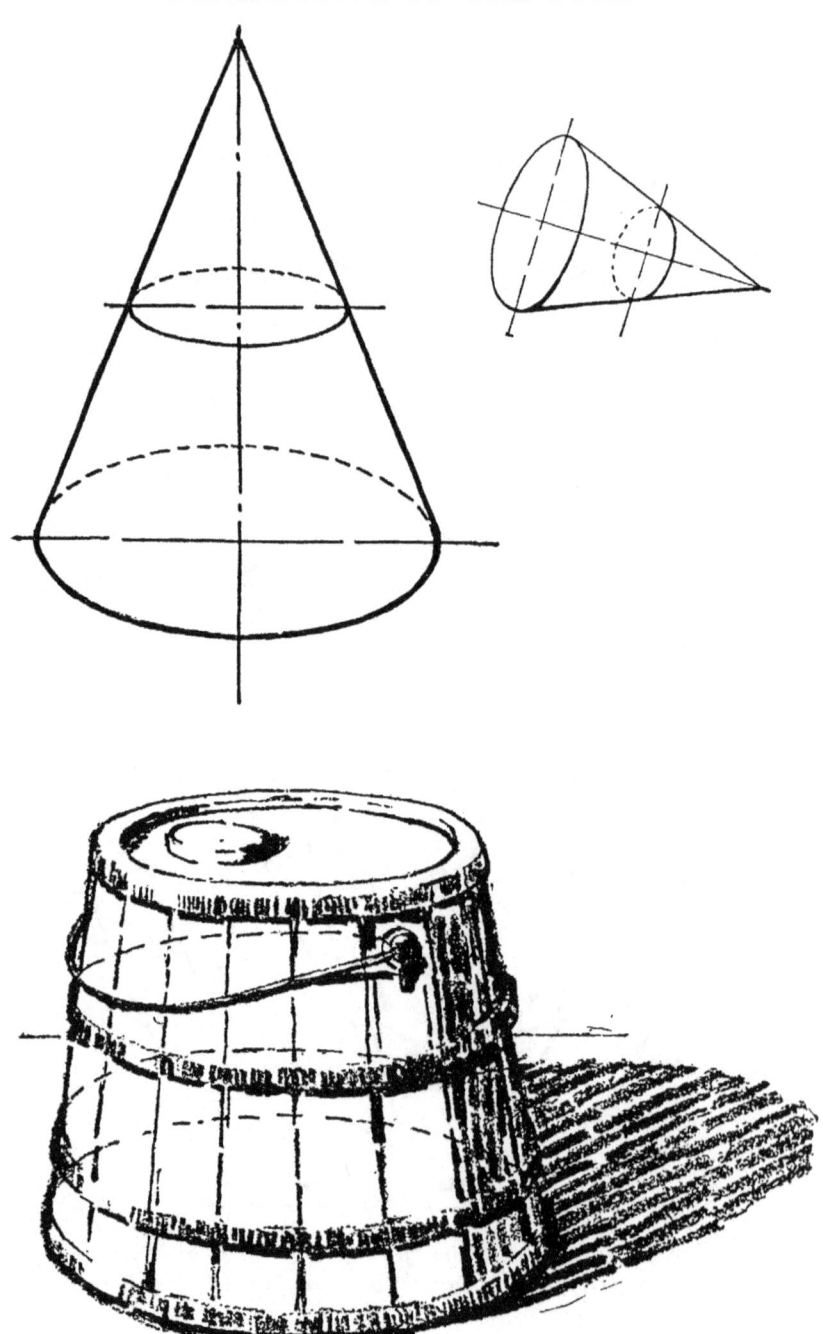

PERSPECTIVE OF THE CONE

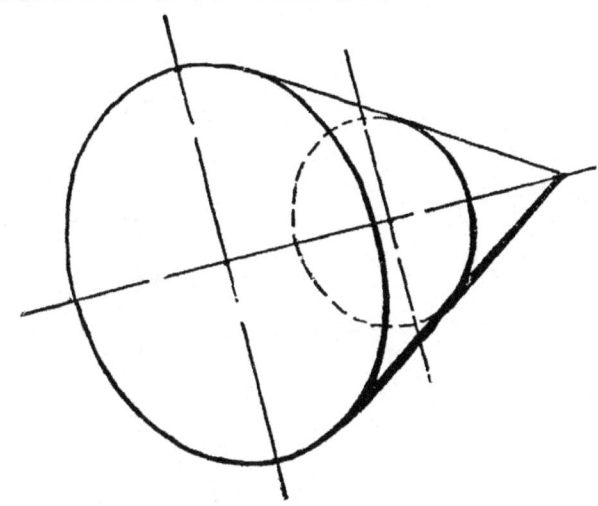

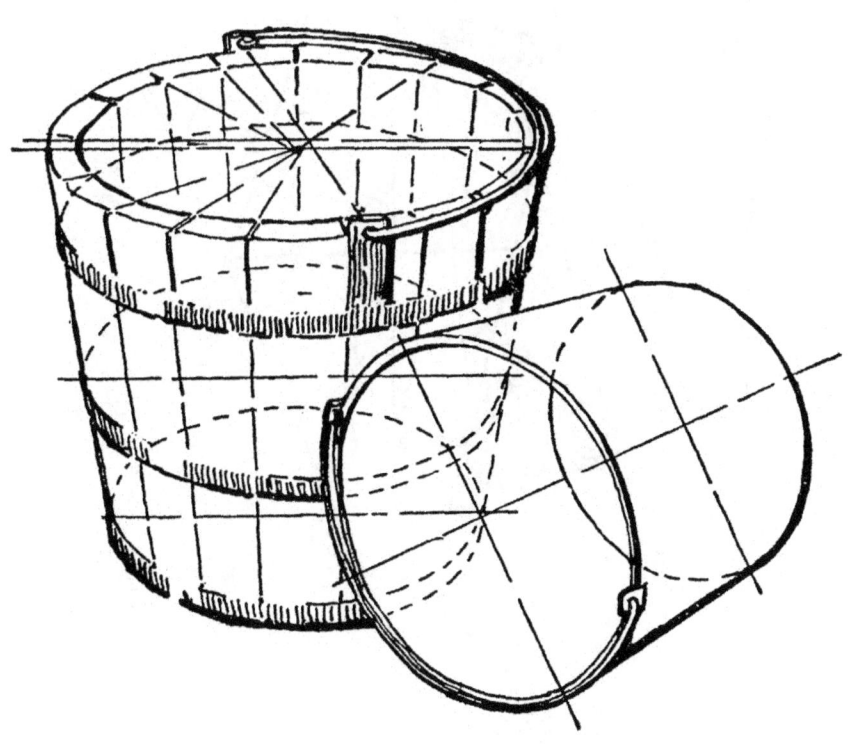

THE SO-CALLED "PICTURE PLANE"

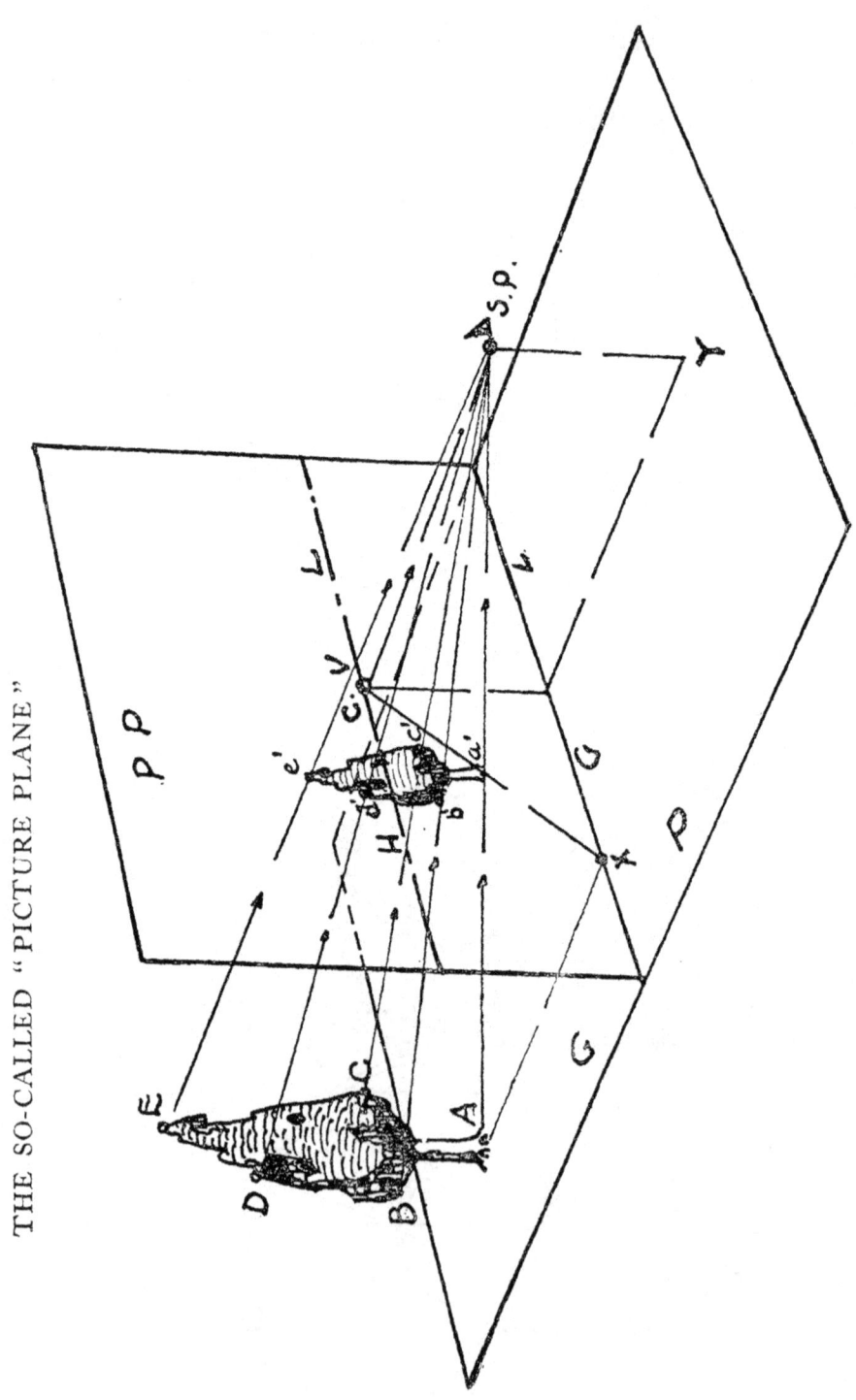

S P = *station point of the observer.* H L = *horizon.* C V = *center of vision.* A, B, C, D, E = *object seen through the picture plane.* a′, b′, c′, d′, e′ = *appearance of the object on the picture plane. Notice that the P P (the picture plane) is perpendicular to* G P (*the ground plane*).

judge and if the drawing appears out of proportion in spite of measurements to the contrary, the drawing must be altered to satisfy the criticism of the eye. Judgment as to proportions is a mental appraisal through the eye, reinforced by careful measurements.

To measure the dimensions of a cube, hold the pencil *at arm's length* toward the object; do not point the pencil toward that object, but hold it in such a manner that it would rest flat against the so-called picture plane.* And then while the pencil is at arm's length, compare the measurement of one part with another part. For example, discover how the breadth of one side compares with its height,—in other words, convince yourself of the ratio and

NOTE B. The "picture plane" is an imaginary vertical plane perpendicular to the line of vision when that line of vision is directed toward the center of vision (which is a point on the horizon directly opposite the eye). If a pane of glass is held in the position of the picture plane, a beginner can quite easily see the perspective of the objects to be drawn, particularly if the pane of glass is framed, like a slate, so that the edges of the frame, vertical and horizontal, will indicate the proper slant of the lines of the object to be drawn.

proportion of any part to any other part that may be in question. Hold the pencil so that the thumb is free to move along it to measure the lengths of whatever sections you may wish to compare.

When several objects are in a group, it is helpful to know how much lower or higher than another one point may appear to be. The straight edge of a paper or of a mahl-stick held horizontally in the direction of the objects will settle any question on this point.

In like manner, when several objects are placed one above another, it is helpful to hold out in the direction of the objects a vertical straightedge to assist in determining the relative distance to left or right that the objects may seem to be.

Books on drawing frequently print exhaustive directions about how to sharpen the pencil, how to hold it, the slant at which shading lines should be drawn, and many other details which in reality are of little or no importance. The fact is that

PERSPECTIVE OF THE CUBE

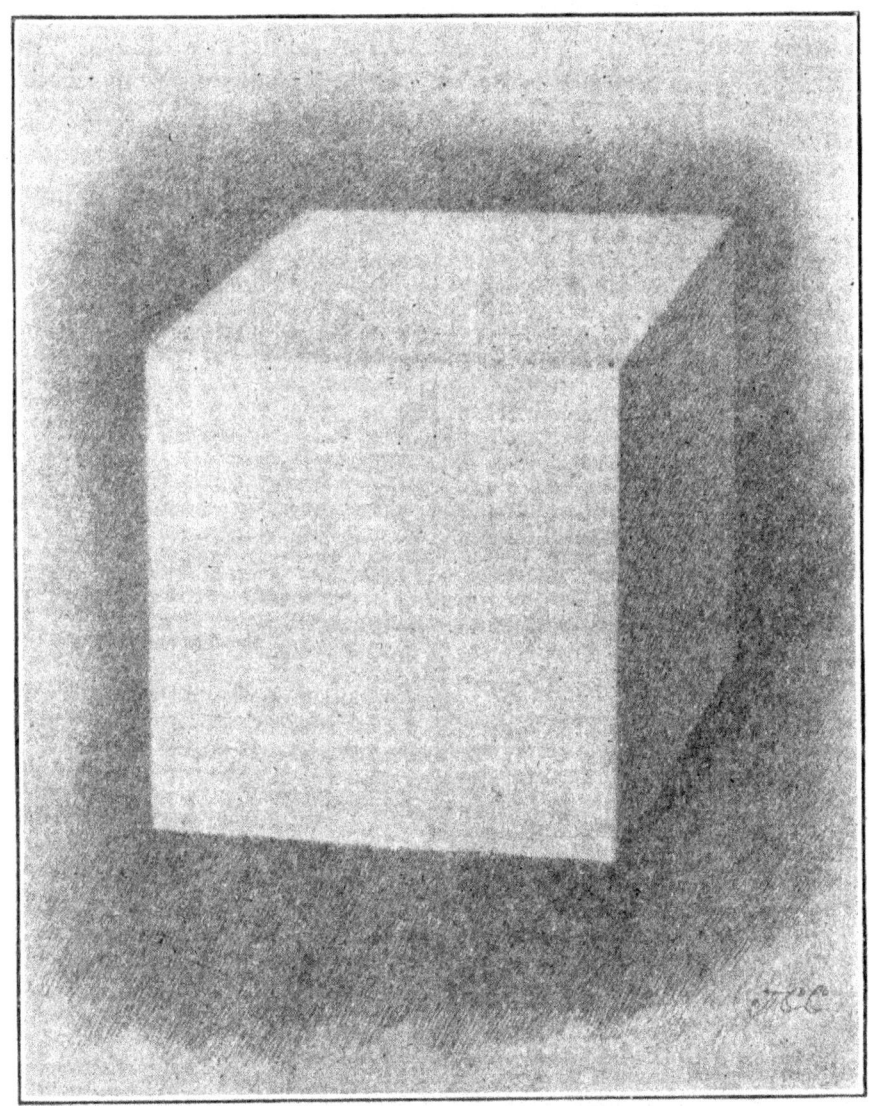

An example of pencil treatment.

PERSPECTIVE OF THE CIRCLE

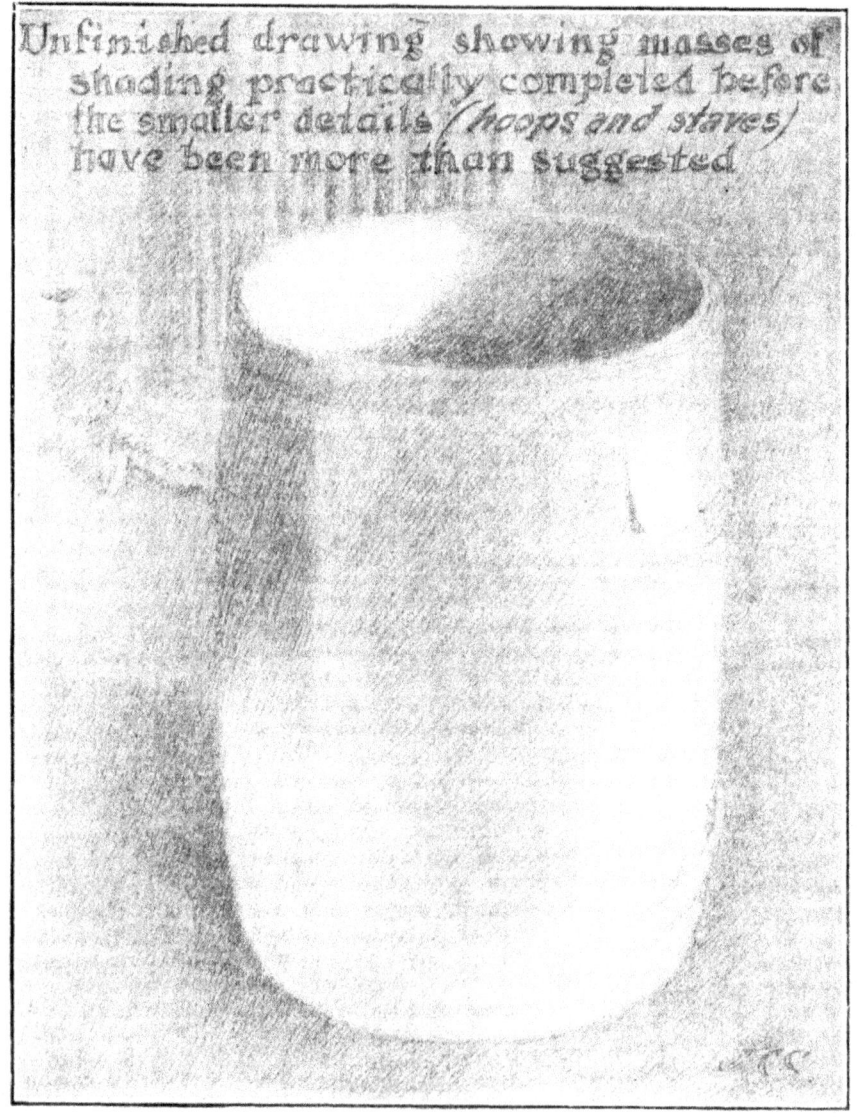

An example of pencil treatment.

an ordinary pencil, if not too hard, fairly sharpened and held in the artist's hand in any way he likes, will suffice.

A beginner will do well for some time to make his drawings with pencil, unless he has an opportunity to study under the direction of a capable teacher who will see that his efforts in charcoal are worth while. For out-door sketching a rather soft pencil upon paper with a slightly rough surface will give excellent results. However, if sketches are afterwards to be inked in, a smoother surface and a pencil about " B " or " No. 2 " is best, because too soft a lead does not receive ink very satisfactorily and dirties the paper so that the preparatory lines are often very hard to erase. Pencil drawings should never be rubbed to produce a gray tone, though charcoal drawings are treated in this manner.

Do not make tiny drawings—their mistakes are not easily discovered and the progress of the student is retarded.

In commencing a drawing of objects

placed in front of the onlooker, the first thing of importance is to be sure that the objects are understood as to form and proportions. It is well for the draughtsman to make up his mind which object in the group or which section of an object, he wishes to make the most important, because to make a drawing or a painting interesting it is essential that there be a point of greatest emphasis. A study may be over-emphasized in every part, both as to drawing and as to modeling in light and shade, with certain beneficial effect to the student, even though the result may be entirely lacking in this principle of dominance and subordination, but such a drawing is sure to prove uninteresting. A group of several pieces of fruit, for instance, may be so drawn that in the result, each piece of fruit forces itself upon the onlooker with equal insistence. Such a drawing may be perfectly good exercise, but it is not a true representation of one's view of the group of fruit, because when one looks at a considerable number of objects at the same time, his interest, and therefore his focus, is not bestowed equally upon each of the pieces at the same time. A particular apple, or perhaps a bunch of grapes, appears to the onlooker more interesting in form and more beautiful in color than any of the other pieces, and so the problem is not, how each piece looks to him as he focuses his attention upon one piece at a time, but rather, how the group looks to him when his attention is focused upon the piece of greatest interest. Thus does the principle of dominance and subordination unconsciously affect every observer, and thus should the artist consciously make use of it.

When the beginner, pencil and paper in hand, faces the objects to be drawn, he instinctively asks, "Where do I begin?" There are so many points at which one might begin, that the answer to this question is not an easy one. It is often a good plan to begin with the largest mass, particularly if it be in the foreground and to put down upon paper the longest or most evident line of that object. In a cube this would be the front vertical line. When this line has been drawn it becomes at once the measuring unit for comparison of length with the other lines.

Beginning at the top of the paper and working gradually downward, or beginning in the upper left-hand corner and working gradually toward the lower right, as sometimes advised, has no advantages over the exactly opposite attack. However, begin at once somewhere with an important line and draw. As soon as a few lines have been lightly made, the draughtsman's eye detects a mistake in proportion or in angle, and at once the correction should be made. Putting down lines and correcting them honestly, quickly, eagerly—thus is a drawing made. The artist must be his own very severe critic. Often an artist is told, "You must be very patient." The fact is, if he were "patient," he would never have become an artist. It is impatience, the *eager* readiness to alter and change, to erase and "try, try again," that produces results in drawing.

If the drawing is to be made in light-and-shade, place the object to be drawn so that its lighting will be simple—that is, so that it is lighted from one side only. The shadows and the lights will then be easiest to see and easiest to express upon paper. A good lighting is absolutely vital. Then do not at the commencement fuss with the smaller sections. Get the large masses suggested in outline as quickly as possible, so that the imagination will have a chance to keep ahead of the hand. The artist acquires an ability to visualize more or less completely, when he begins his drawing, the finished work upon the paper. This vision, if you will call it that, makes the result seem possible and urges him on to the completion of his work.

Remember always that a line, placed

upon the paper, is only suggested, only tentative, only on trial. Draw lightly these first lines and feel always how easy it is to correct and change, and to make more beautiful. Depend upon your eye; measure if you will and as much as you will, but remember that all " in the air " measurements are necessarily inaccurate and correct without hesitation mistakes as fast as you discover them.

OBLIQUE PERSPECTIVE

OBLIQUE PERSPECTIVE

This is not essential to the beginner, but he will do well to try to understand it.

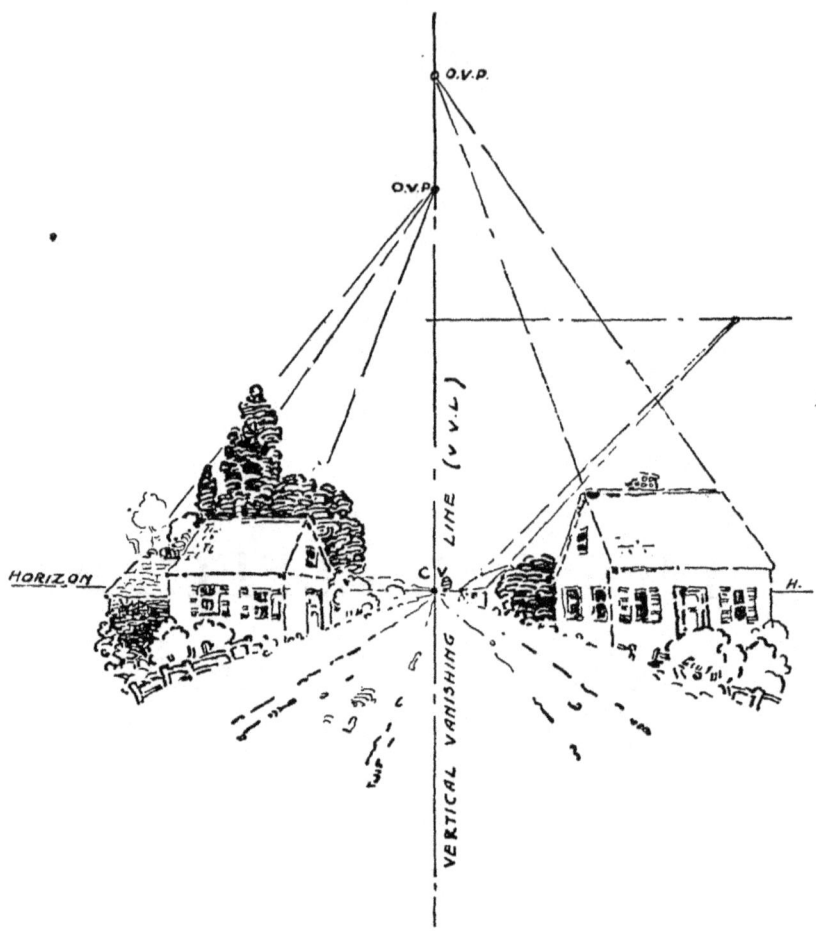

Some parts of buildings, such as slanting roofs, are in oblique perspective. In this illustration the ends of the buildings facing the street are in vertical planes which are parallel to each other. Those planes converge toward a vertical vanishing line (V.V.L.) All sets of parallel lines lying in those planes converge toward certain points (O.V.P. = oblique vanishing point) on the vertical line.

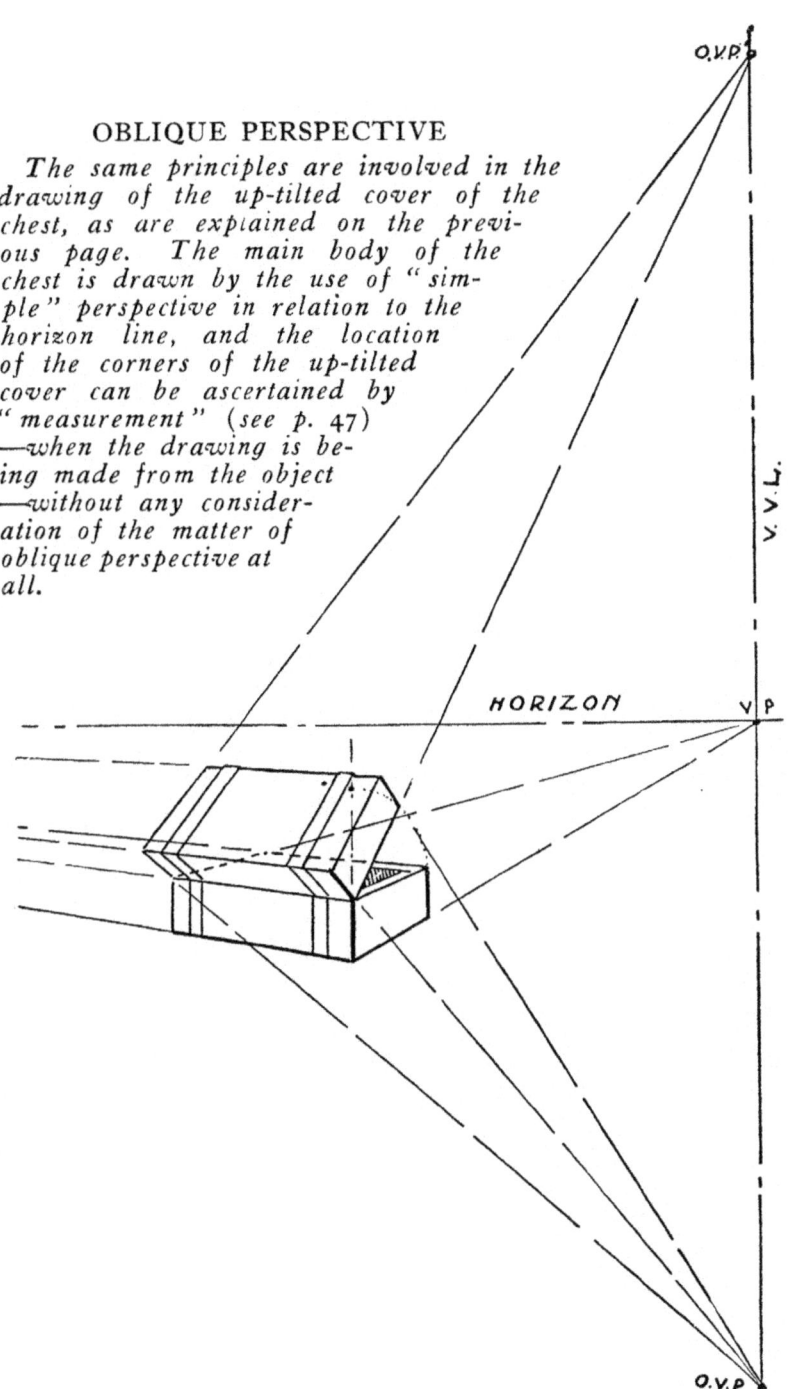

OBLIQUE PERSPECTIVE

The same principles are involved in the drawing of the up-tilted cover of the chest, as are explained on the previous page. The main body of the chest is drawn by the use of " simple" perspective in relation to the horizon line, and the location of the corners of the up-tilted cover can be ascertained by " measurement " (see p. 47) —when the drawing is being made from the object —without any consideration of the matter of oblique perspective at all.

O.V.P.

V.V.L.

HORIZON

V P

O.V.P

MEDIUM AND TREATMENT

MEDIUM AND TREATMENT

PENCIL is the easiest medium for the beginner. A great variety of tones can be produced with it, and it is usually easy to erase, so that the draughtsman feels unafraid. It is suitable, however, for only small drawings.

Pen-and-ink is perhaps the most difficult of mediums. It is definitely and unqualifiedly black. Unless the draughtsman has acquired considerable skill, the result of his effort betrays cruelly his every fault of draughtsmanship and treatment. It is a medium for line expression, or for solid black masses. "Cross-hatching" to produce the effect of middling tones is almost never anything but crude and disappointing.

Charcoal, after a little study, is perhaps the easiest of the mediums adapted to large areas. It permits of individual treatment, and is what is called a " sensitive medium," responding to the vigorous or to the caressing touch of the draughtsman. It is seldom used as a " line medium."

Colored chalks, or pastels, are somewhat more difficult of manipulation than charcoal, and require an understanding of color.

Water-color paint is of two kinds: transparent and opaque (tempera). The handling of transparent water color is extremely difficult. Black and white water color is much used as an illustrator's medium. Ordinarily the drawing is first laid out in pencil and the washes of water color are laid on afterward. Two excellent examples of treatment are shown on pages 77 and 79. Tempera, or opaque water color, is particularly well adapted to poster work, and since the washes can be put on in flat opaque tones, the student will find this a very grateful medium. The poster on page 81 is a fine example.

Black and white oil paint is much used for illustration and is a very satisfactory medium for that work. It has the advantage of remaining the same in tone after it dries, while water color becomes somewhat different in tone after it dries.

The example of various treatments in different mediums that follow from page 67 to page 87, will indicate to the student that there is a great variety of ways by which the draughtsman may portray whatever objects he wishes to draw.

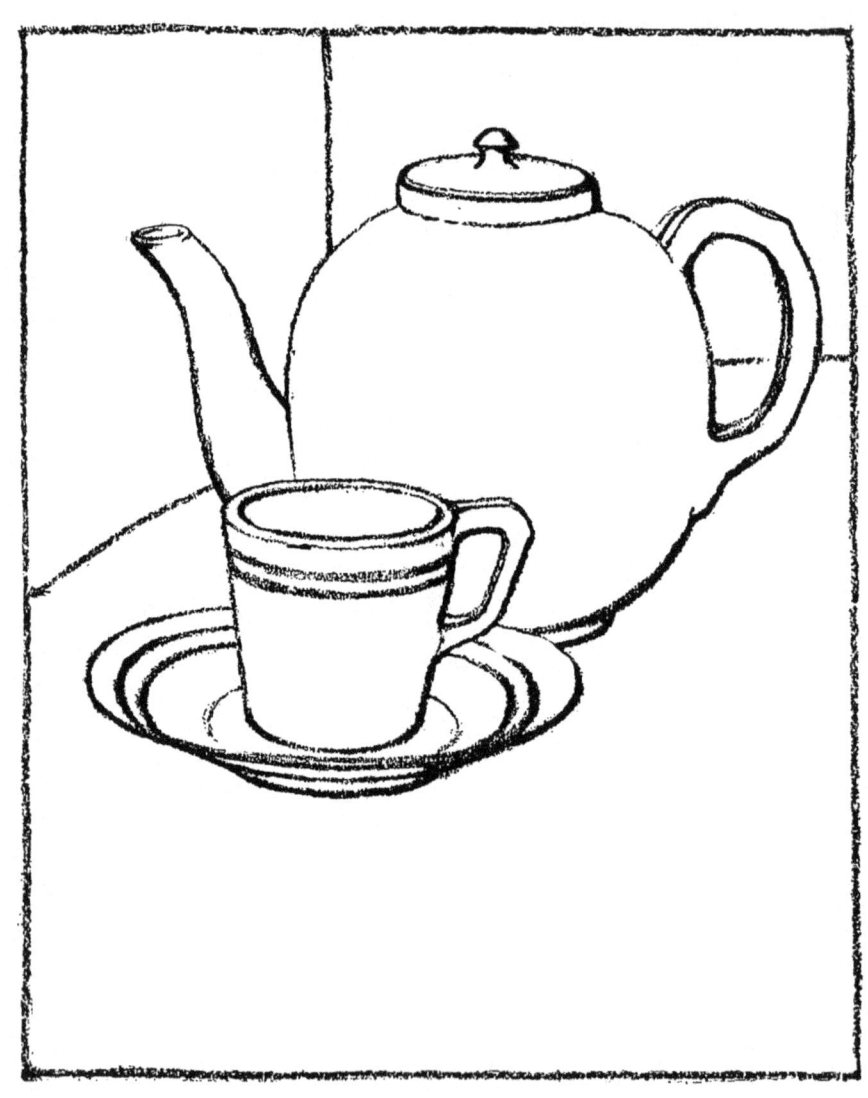

1. *Still-life group rendered in accented outline.*
Pencil treatment.

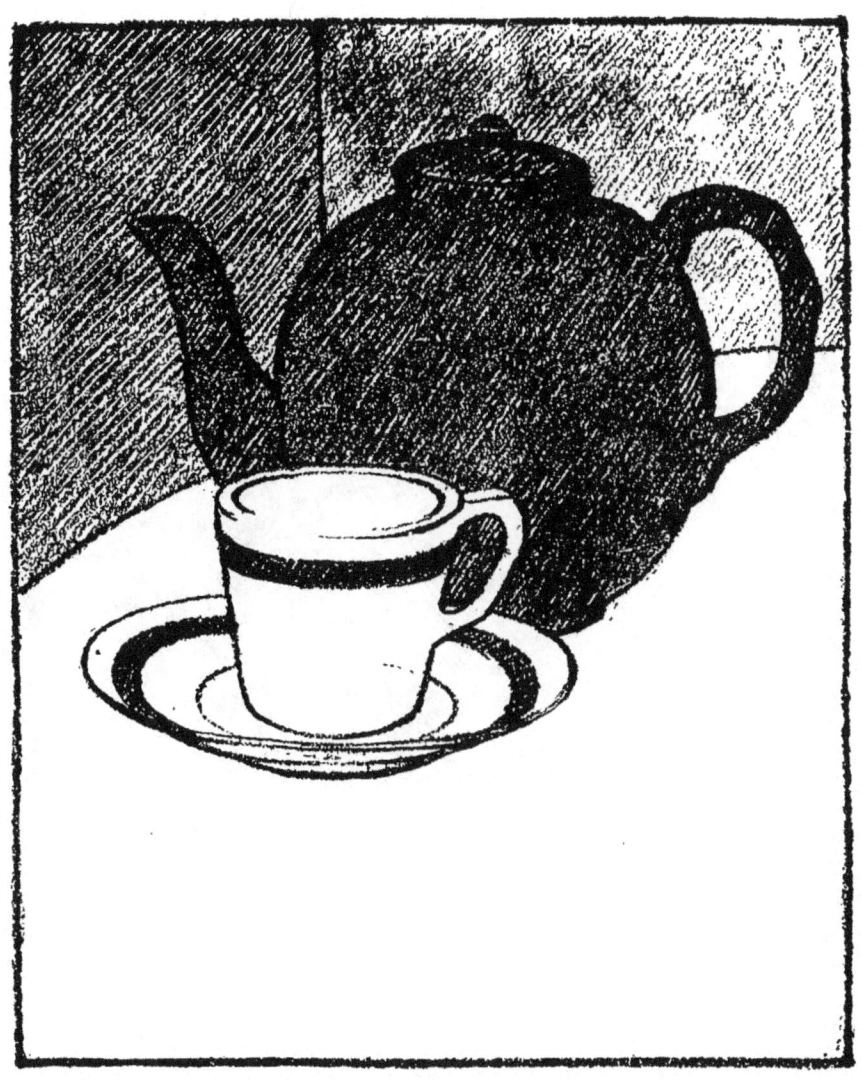

2. *Same still-life group rendered in flat values. Pencil treatment.*

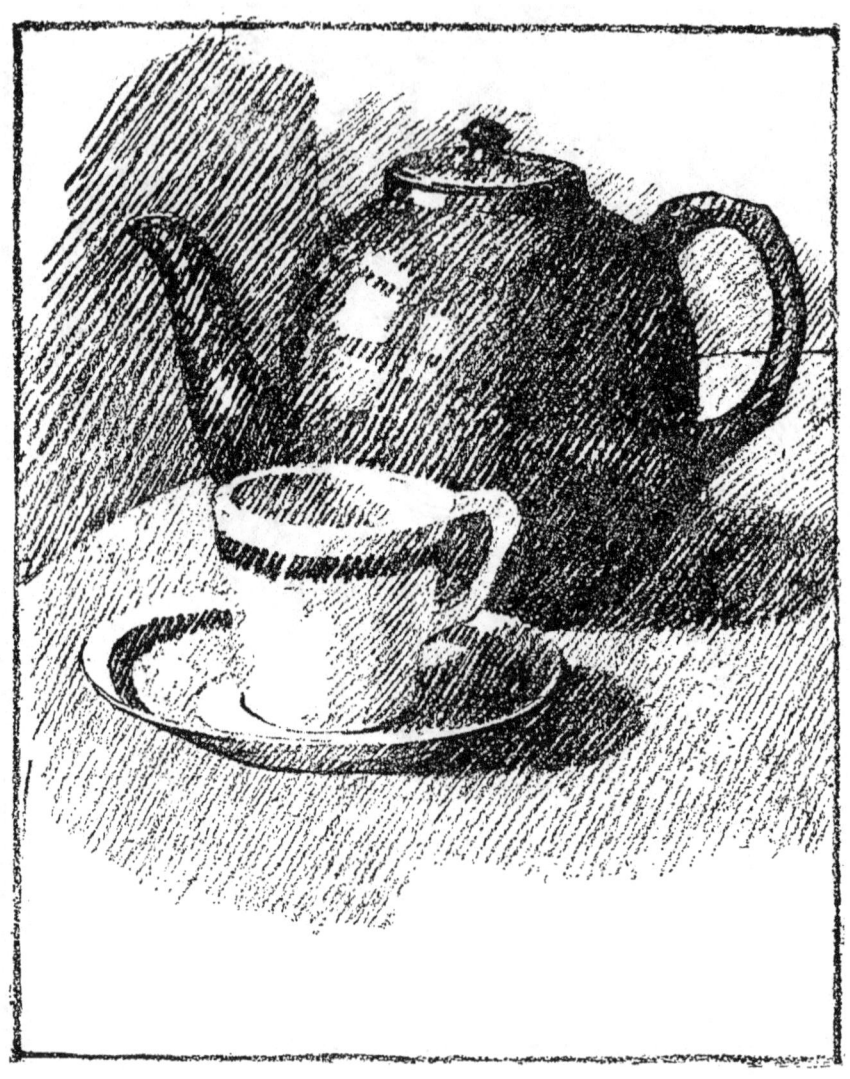

3. *The same still-life group rendered in light and shade.*
Pencil treatment.

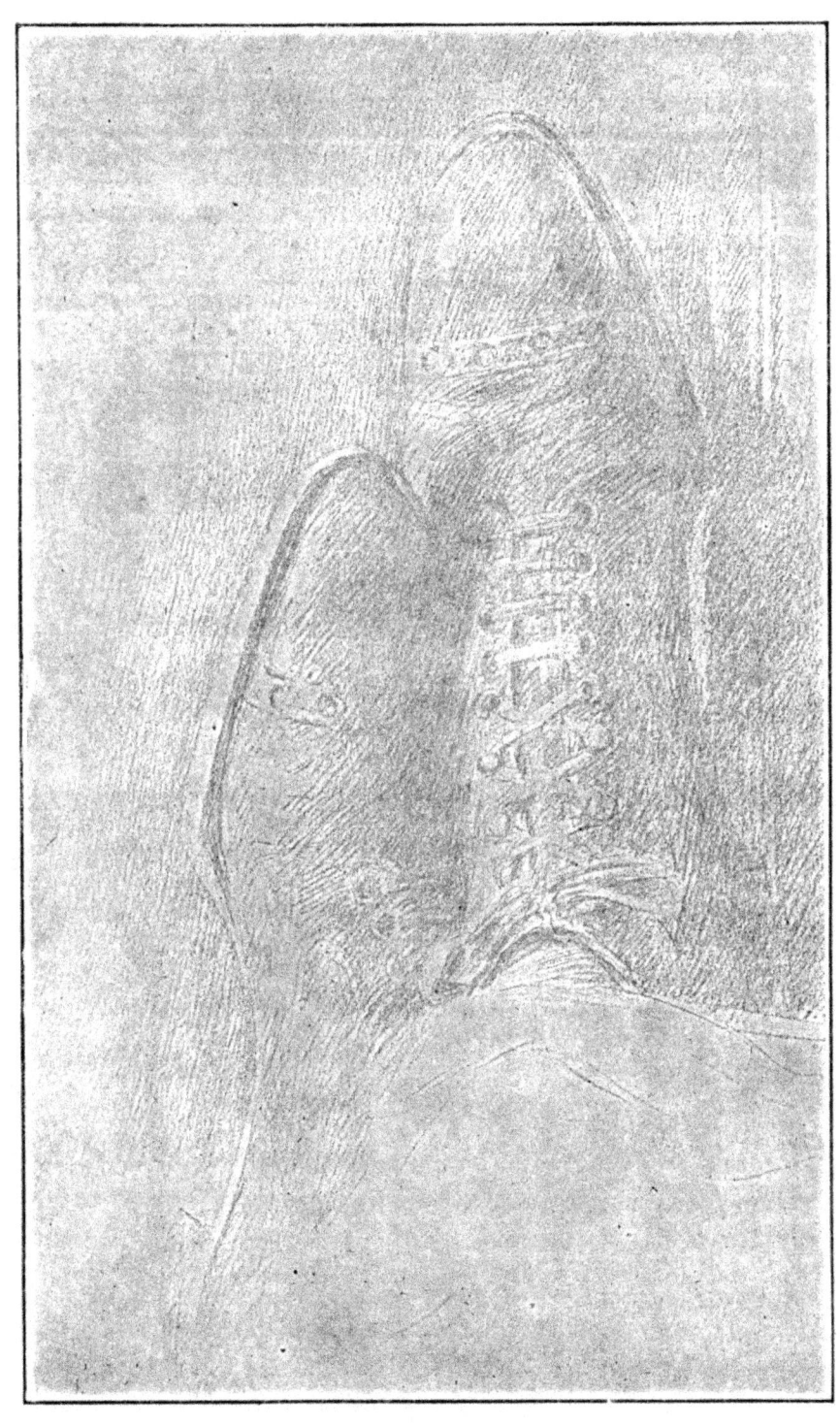

An example of pencil treatment by J. C. C.

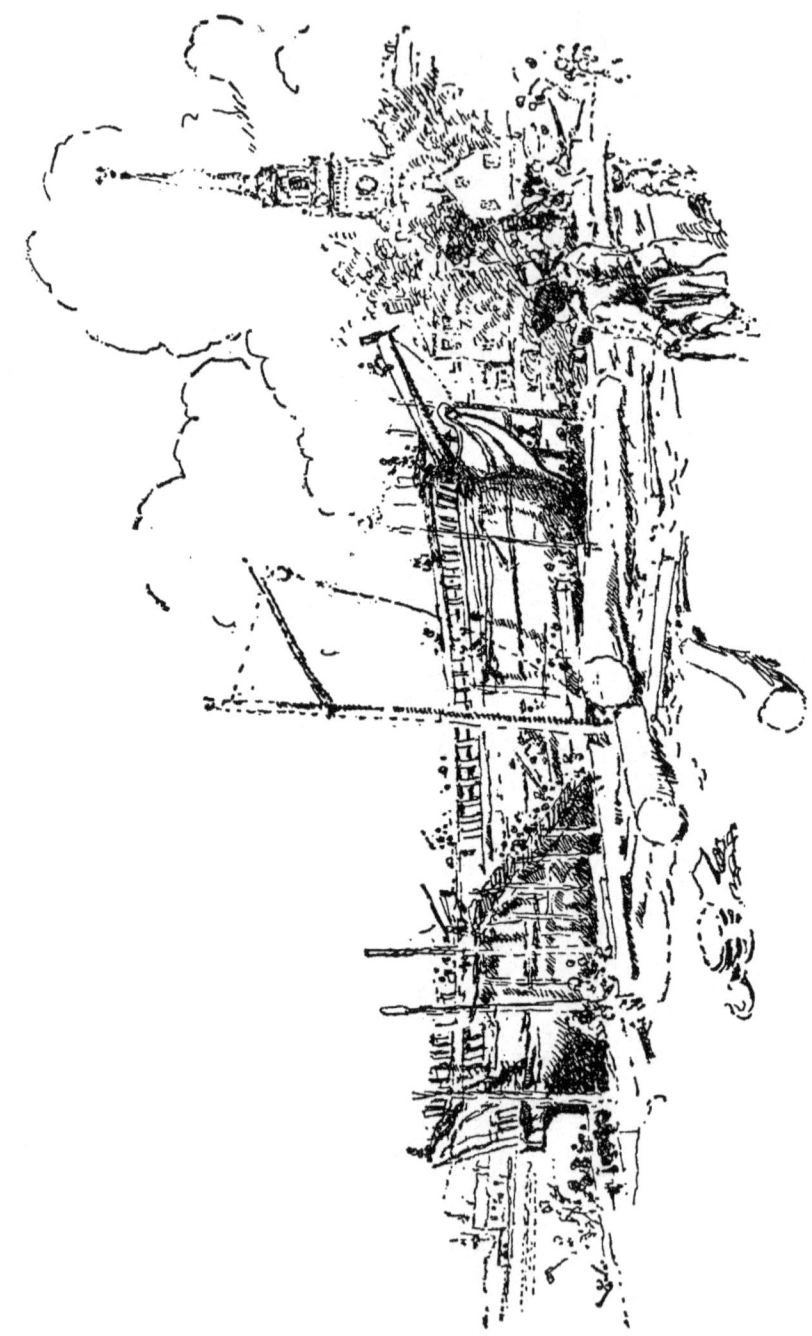

An example of pen and ink treatment by John Walcott Adams.

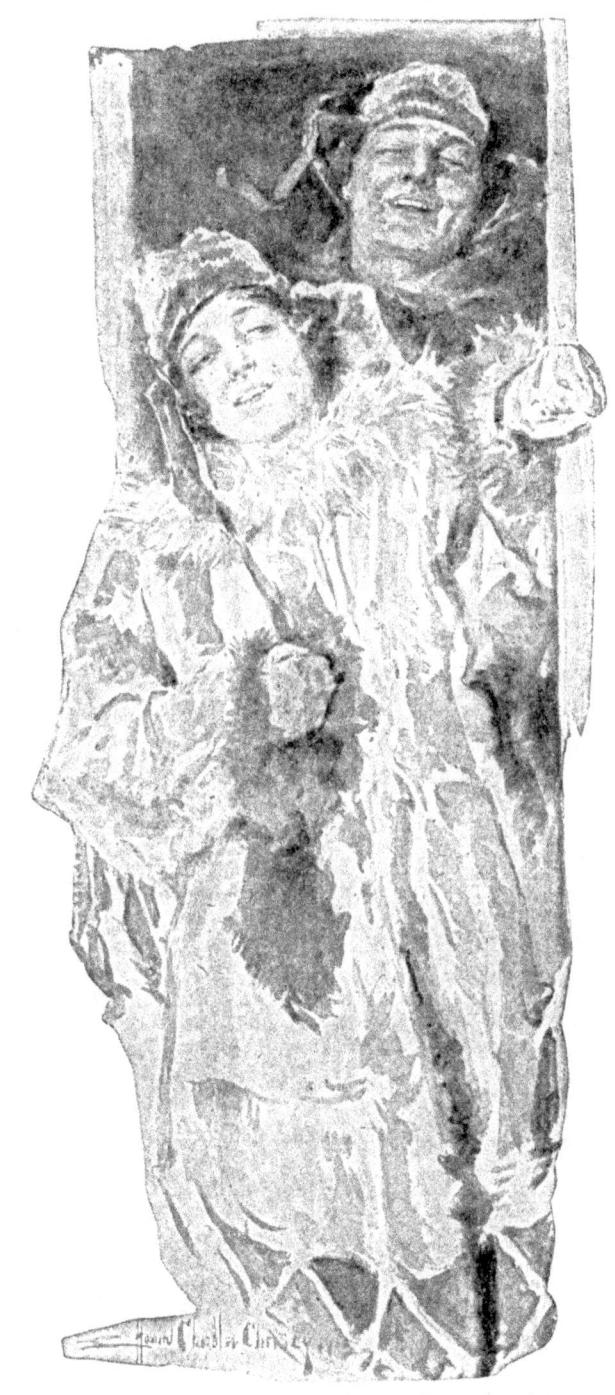

An example of wash drawing, by Howard Chandler Christy. The medium is black and white water-color paint.

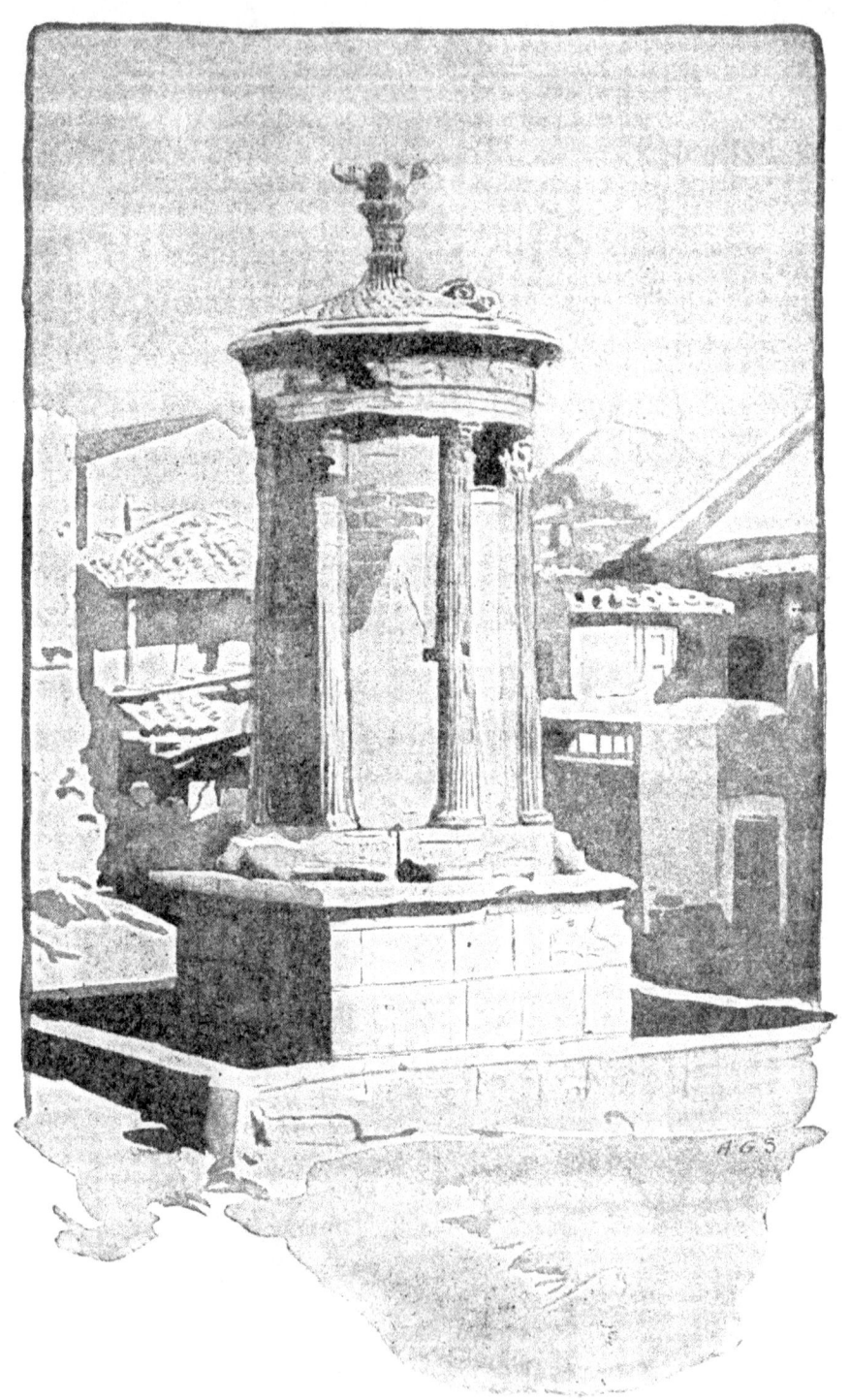

*A wash drawing made with India ink and water by
A. G. Schulman.*

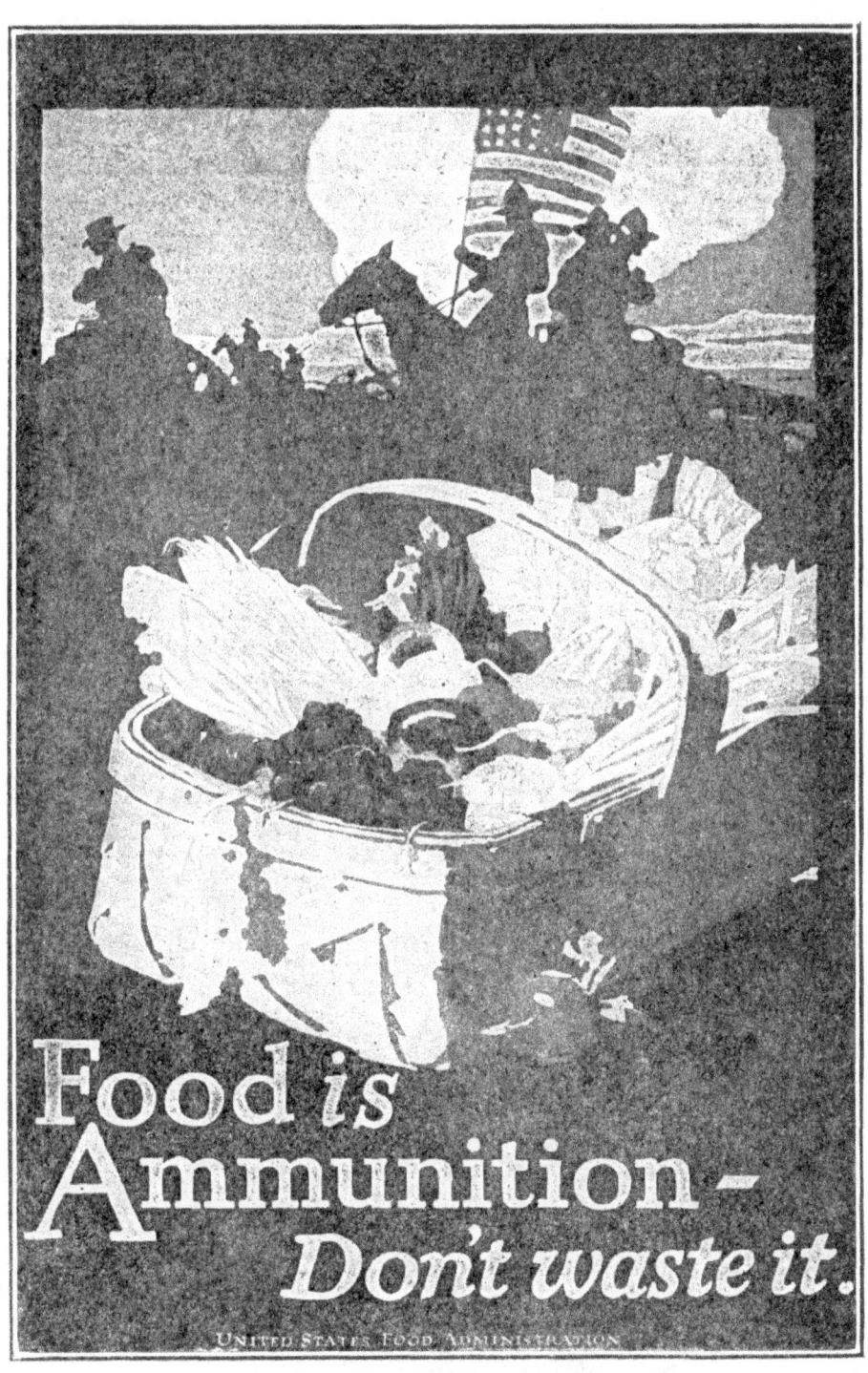

An example of poster treatment. The medium is opaque water-color paint, called "tempera." The artist is John E. Sheridan.

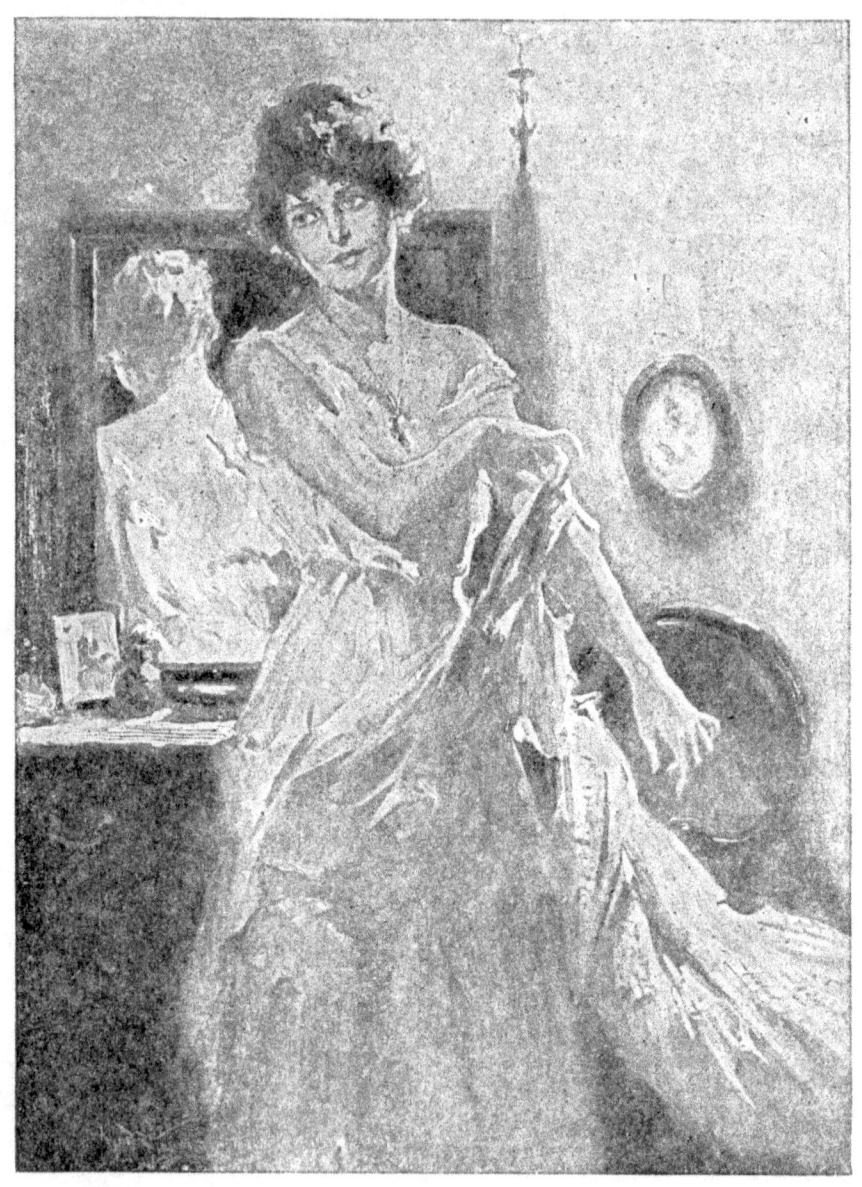

*The medium is black and white oil paint.
An illustration by W. D. Stevens.*

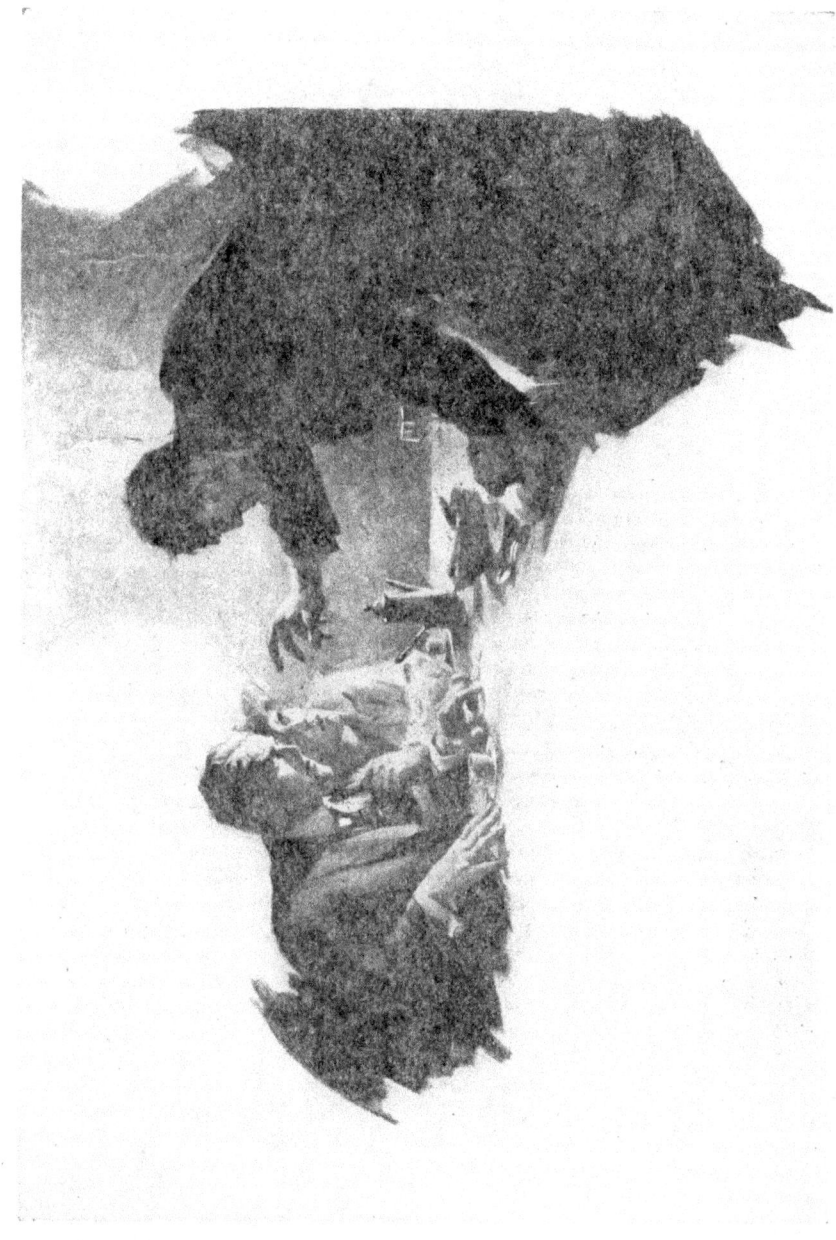

The medium is black and white oil paint. An illustration by Dalton Stevens.

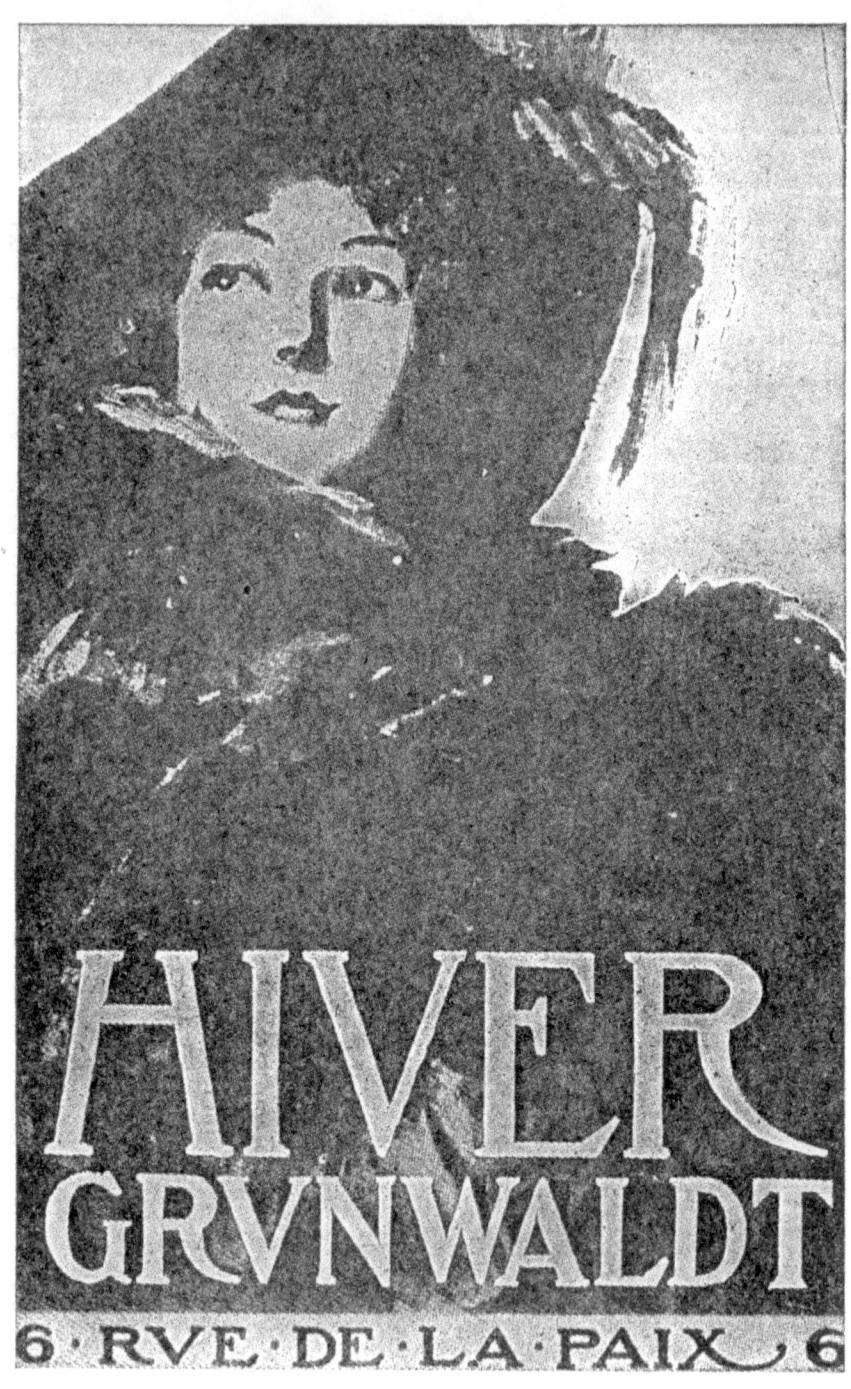

Poster treatment with black and red oil paint by J. C. C.

PICTORIAL COMPOSITION

PICTORIAL COMPOSITION

WE have discussed the use of perspective, and also the manner of measuring to convince oneself of how the objects to be drawn appear to the draughtsman, and we will now consider briefly that part of art called " pictorial composition," the understanding of which is of the utmost importance. We have said that the " accuracy of drawing is a matter of mathematics," and that a drawing may be precisely accurate and yet not be a thing of art. *Design,* however, is inseparably associated with art and is essentially a part of art itself.

There are two kinds of design — that of two dimensions, called applied or decorative, and that of three dimensions, which

DEFECTIVE COMPOSITIONS

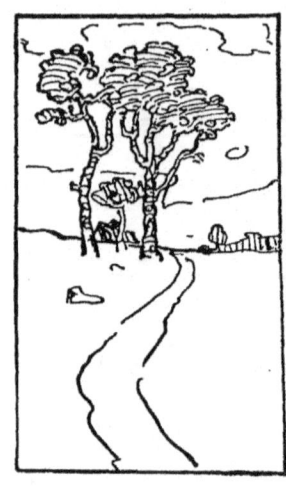
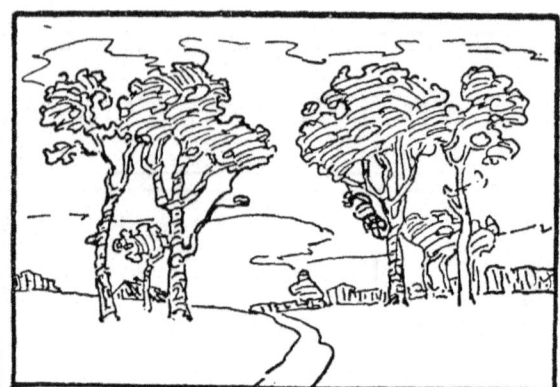

1. *Defective because the horizon is in the middle of the rectangle.*
2. *Defective because there are two motives of equal importance competing for attention.*

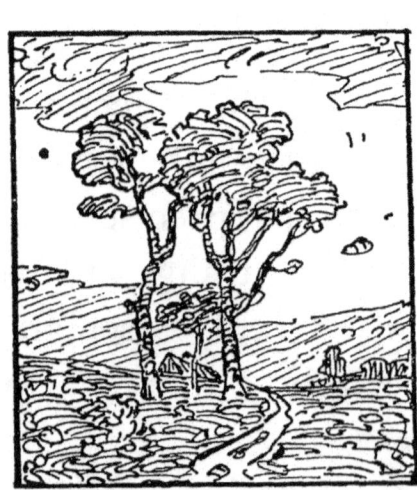
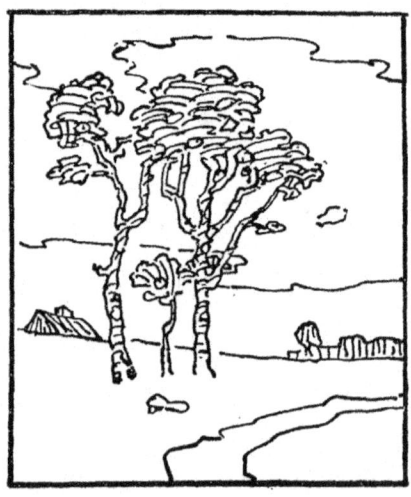

3. *Not bad, but the principal motive is too near center of picture.*
4. *Defective because of lack of harmony among the elements: the house is badly placed, the road is leading out of the picture instead of toward the principal mass.*
Notice on the next page the dignified manner in which the principal mass commands attention.

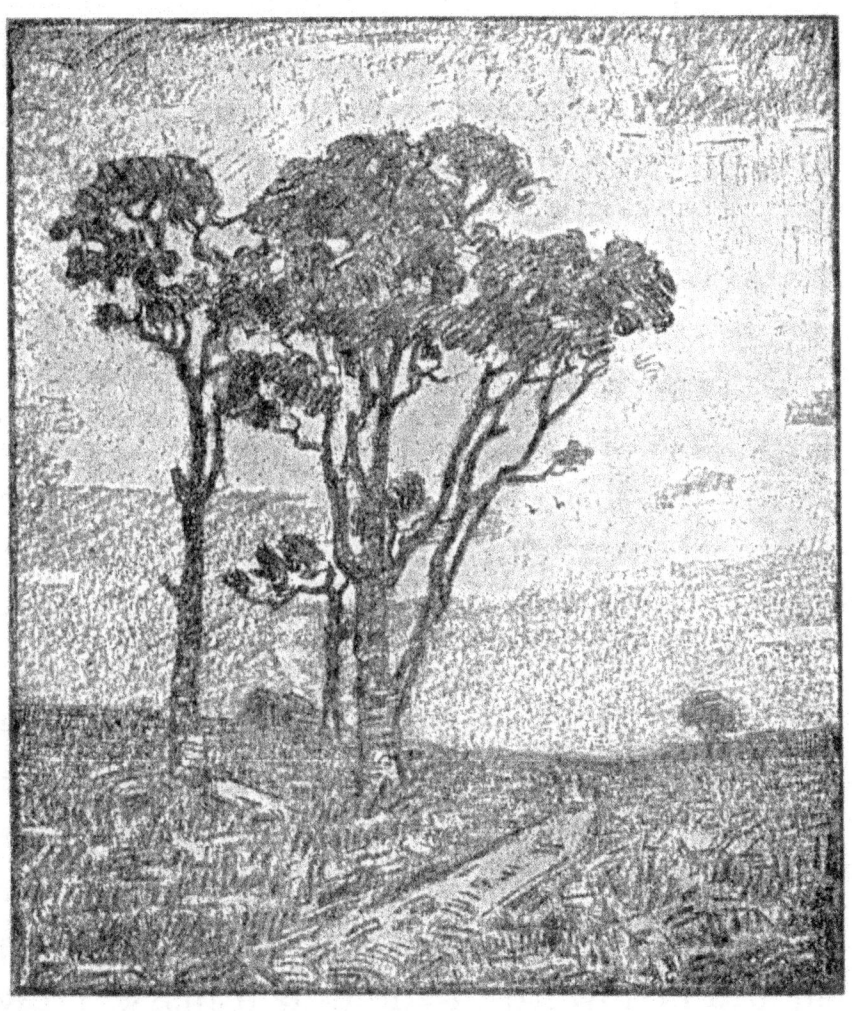

5. *Sunset. Rendered in charcoal. The tree mass domi-nates, the house adds to the mass, the roadway leads up to it, and the background lightens in such a way as to emphasize it.*

is called constructive. It is the former which has to do with picture making and that part of it which has so to do we call pictorial composition. In the study of pictorial composition we learn of possible arrangements of masses of light and dark, arrangements of lines, arrangements of colors within any given space, so that when we are confronted with the problem of drawing a group of still life within a certain rectangle, or the sketching of a landscape within a certain rectangle, we are aware of certain things to avoid and of certain fundamental rules which are absolute: for instance, that idea of dominance and subordination before referred to and already explained. The landscape on page 93 clearly shows the effectiveness of this principle, illustrating the fact that the tendency of other motives in a composition should be toward the dominant mass. How much better is the composition on page 93 with the roadway swinging toward the dominant mass than it would be if the roadway came in at the bottom of the rectangle and ran out at the side without having any relationship to the dominant mass, which in this case is the tree mass.

In this connection let us emphasize the fact that to make beautiful any composi-

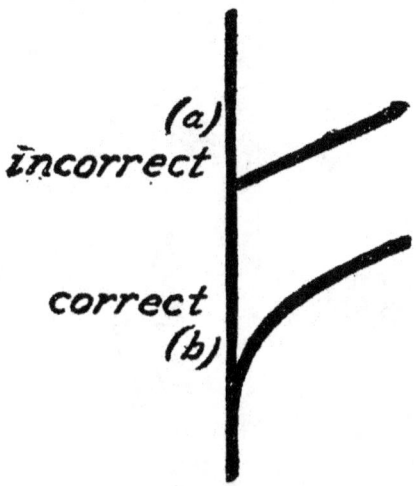

tion, landscape or otherwise, it is necessary that the silhouette shape of each object which is defined in the composition be beautiful. It is just as positively important, although not so often realized, that the contour of the background spaces shall be as beautiful as the silhouette shapes of the objects themselves.

By arranging the lines of a drawing in

such a way that there is as little evident crossing of them as possible, we carry out a certain principle which is called *tangen-*

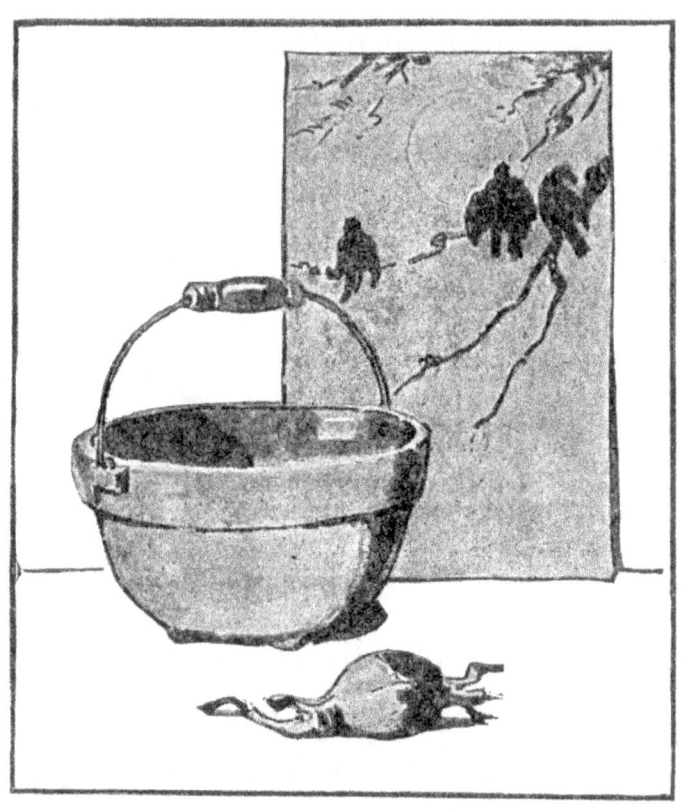

1. *Defective. Shapes and arrangement good, but objects not harmonious. It is absurd to combine a beautiful Japanese print with a cooking utensil and radishes.*

tial junction. (This principle is evident in plant growth.) See page 95.

Another principle is *harmony,* which has

to do with tone, color, and line. "It consists in shunning differences too pro-

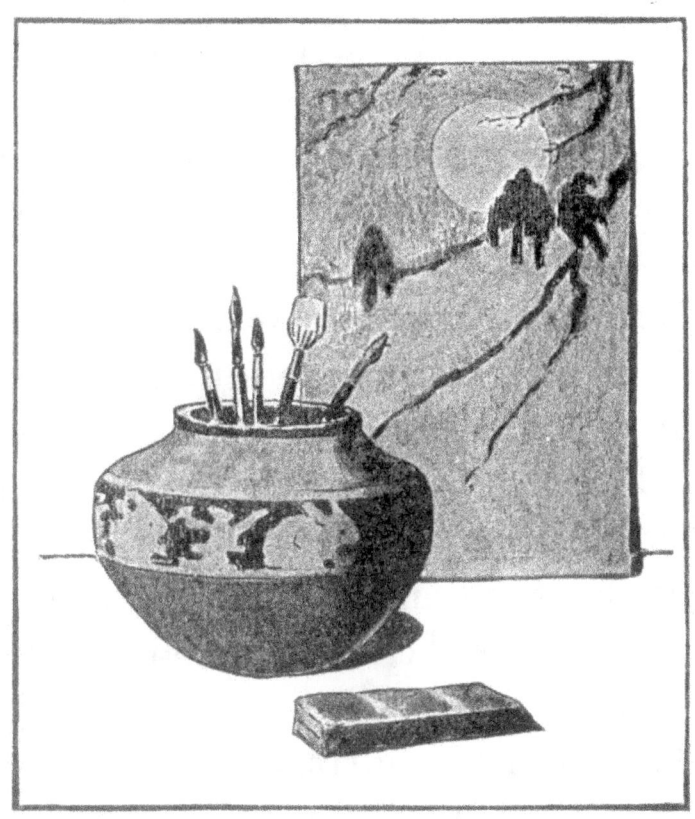

2. *Same arrangement, and shapes much the same as in No. 1. This group is harmonious not only as to shapes but to kinds of objects as well.*

nounced, contrasts too startling. Uniformity of details, tone, measure, and shape, might be defined as perfect harmony. But uniformity is assuredly not the most pleasing manifestation of harmony. The eye craves contrast, variety; how far to go, where to stop, is the problem of the designer," —Batchelder. The composition used as a frontispiece in this book illustrates admirably the correct understanding of this principle.

There are *certain mistakes of arrangement* in pictorial composition frequently made by beginners. Some are here noted. (a) The placing of the horizon of a landscape directly across the middle of a rectangle is an unfortunate start for any picture. Place the horizon above or below the middle.

(b) Too many horizontal lines in a picture have a tendency to give a feeling of separated parts, although strangely enough, vertical lines do not seem to annoy in that way.

(c) Symmetry, while being an excellent thing in the forming of motives (figures) for surface patterns, is quite out of place

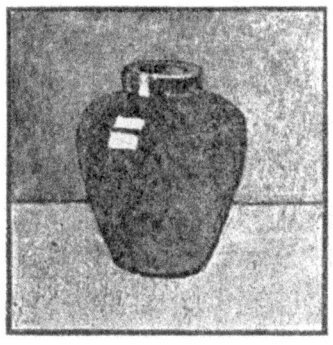 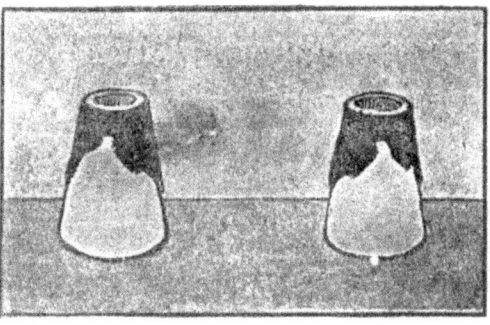

1. *Defective because in center of rectangle.*
2. *Defective because interest is divided by use of symmetry.*

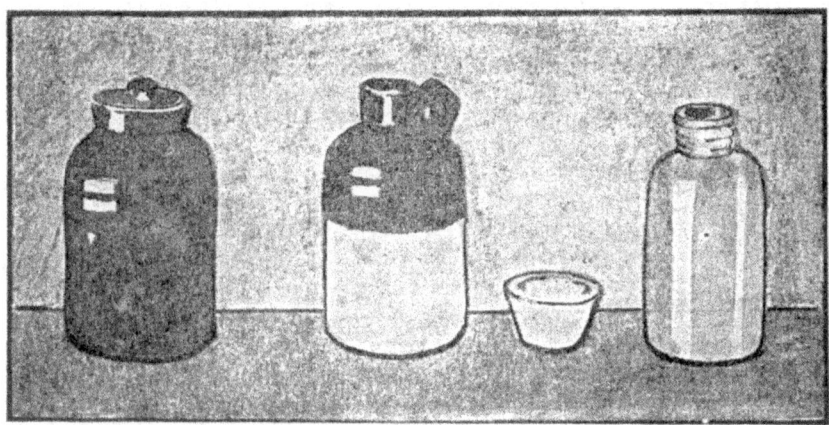

3. *Defective because interest is scattered.*

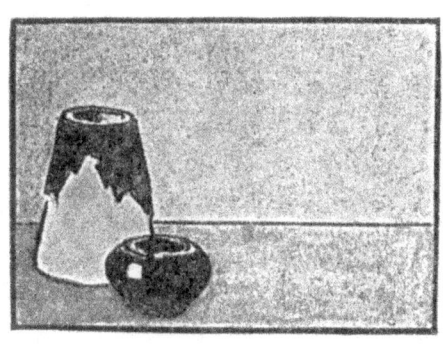 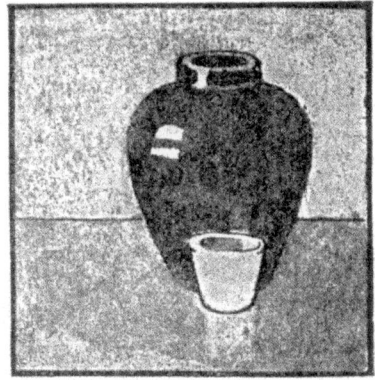

4. *Defective because of lack of balance.*
5. *Defective because of lack of balance and lack of interest.*

in a pictorial composition. For example, in No. 2 on page 92 the trees placed as they are at the left and the right of the picture, being of similar size and tone, divide the interest and produce ineffectiveness, whereas No. 5 on the next page, with one large tree mass dominating and the other tree subordinated, produces an effect that is dignified and altogether pleasing.

The frontispiece shows a number of trees so arranged that there is contrast and variety, but the interest is not scattered.

Pictorial Composition

Proportions of rectangles generally used by professional painters.

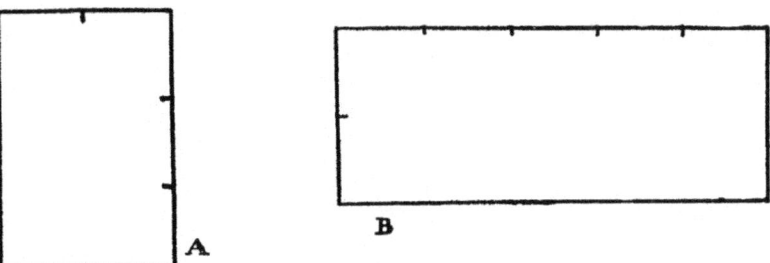

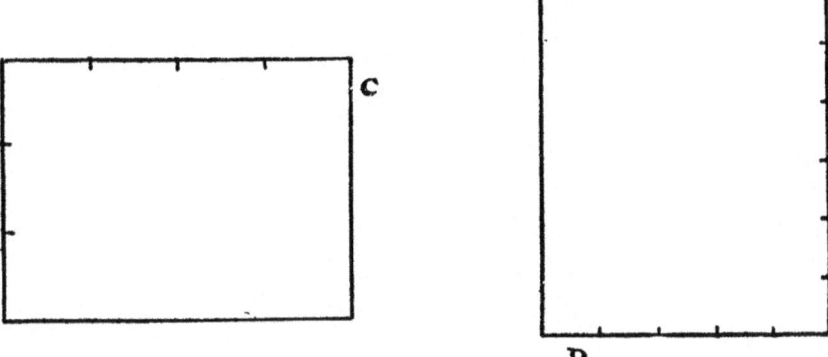

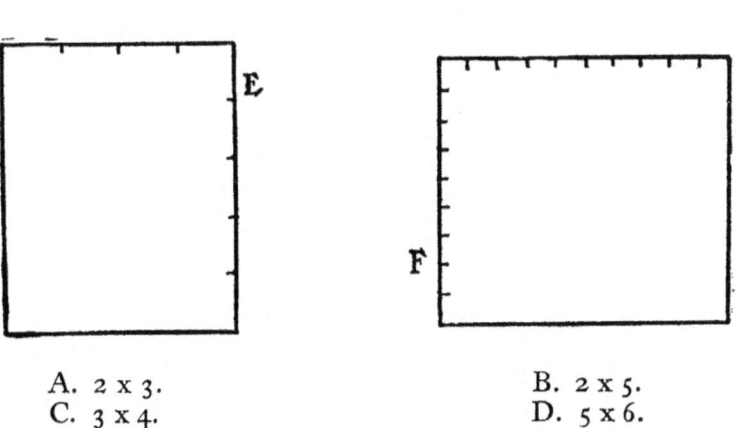

A. 2 x 3.
C. 3 x 4.
E. 4 x 5.

B. 2 x 5.
D. 5 x 6.
F. 9 x 10.

LETTERING

LETTERING

A KNOWLEDGE of lettering is so often useful to the artist, — beginner or professional, and so little is known of the subject by the average student, that this chapter is here added.

There are certain liberties which may be taken with some of the letters of the alphabet without spoiling their classic proportions, but there is never any excuse for making so-called " fancy " letters. Eccentric and caricatured letters may sometimes be useful in advertisements when those advertisements are in the behalf of goods which are very inexpensive, such as chewing gum, but even then it is doubtful if anything can be gained by the malformation of letters. Certainly, if the article for sale is high priced, such as an automobile or a victrola, there is no room for doubt that the lettering of these advertisements demands the greatest consideration of classic style.

In advertisements lettering must be in keeping with the commodity advertised. Obviously, perfumery advertisements should have graceful lettering, while an advertisement for traction engines calls for solidly constructed, weighty letters; but whether the letters are graceful or weighty, they must be properly proportioned and spaced.

Much harm has been done by the manner in which lettering has been taught in many of the public schools. Too often the teacher has explained to students that the *linear* space between each two letters of a word must be the same in a line of lettering, and he has directed his pupils to mark off a line for lettering, indicating a certain amount of width for each letter and also a certain amount of unvarying linear space between each two letters. It is obvious that when pupils proceed to construct each letter within a space thus marked out, the resultant line of lettering will present an uneven and awkward appearance, inasmuch as letters such as capital L followed by capital T, or capital A followed by capital W, will prove to be in appearance very much more widely separated from one another than in instances such as where capital N is followed by capital I or capital H is followed by capital E. The fact is that good lettering depends absolutely upon this theory: *The space-area between each two letters of a word must be the same,* and in order to make this possible, round letters must be spaced much closer to one another than the so-called vertical letters.

Note the admirable lettering of the words, " Harper's Magazine " in the title lettered by A. W. Rushmore, on page 110. Here Roman letters are so disposed that the spacing is unusually distinguished, pos-

AABCDEEFG
HIJJKKKLM
MMNNOOP
PQQQRRRSS
TTUVVWYZ

"ROMAN" LETTERS—CAPITALS, OR UPPER CASE.

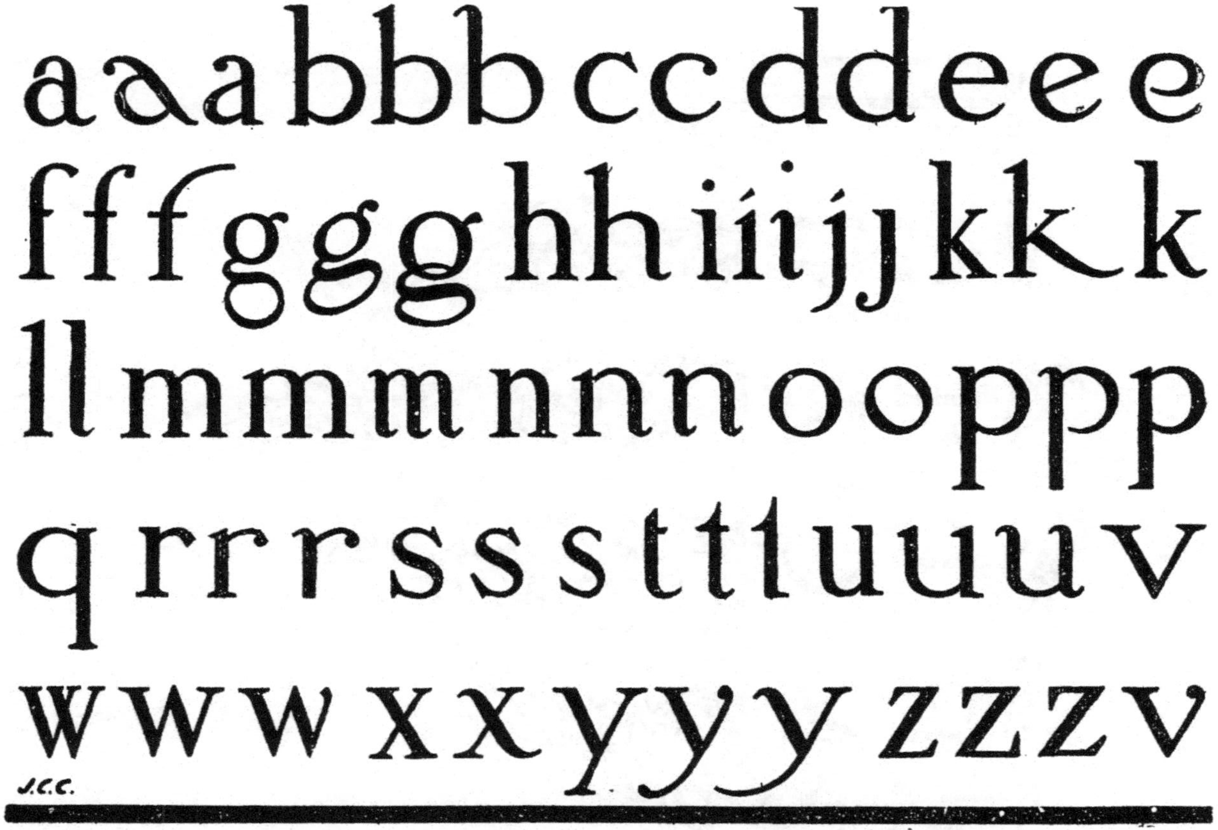
a a a b b b c c d d e e e
f f f g g g h h i i i j j k k k
l l m m m n n n o o p p p
q r r r s s s t t t u u u v
w w w x x y y y z z z v
J.C.C.

"ROMAN" LETTERS—SMALL, OR LOWER CASE.

sessing dignity, simplicity, and style. Notice how closely the A follows the H,

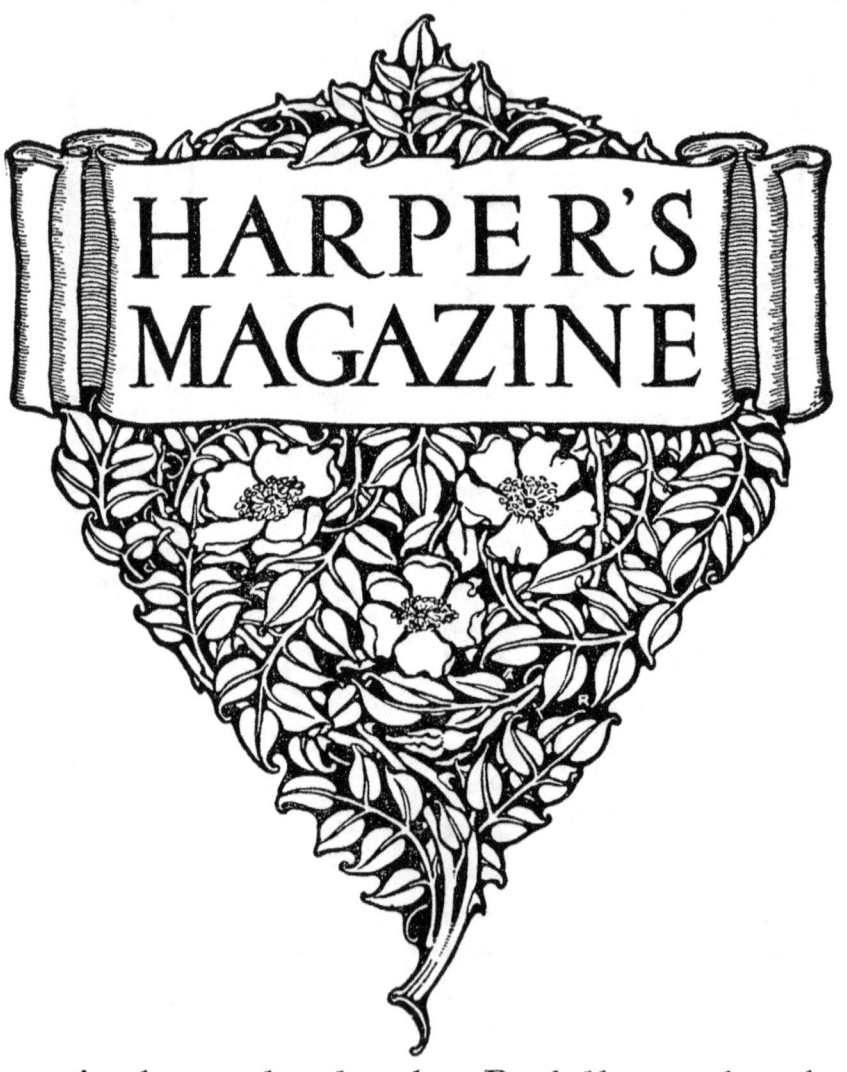

again how closely the R follows the A;
then notice that between the E and the R
there is a much greater spacing to allow

a background space-area between the letters to correspond with those spaces between the letters, H, A, and R.

Remember then that the letterer who is worthy of the name so constructs and so places his letters as to make, as nearly as possible, an equal distribution of space-area between each two letters. This enables the reader's eye to run smoothly along the line without any interruptions, except those intended to separate words and sentences. It is true that a goodly amount of space between words in a line makes that line more legible, but contrary to what one might expect, too great a space between letters in the same word makes the line less legible. On page 112 are two lines showing the words "WAY HOME." The first line is a hand-lettered title for a book jacket by Mr. Rushmore. The letters are made very close in order that they may be as large as possible within the specified width. The second line shows the largest letters the printer could use in the same specified width. Notice how separated are the first three letters in the second case, and also notice how much larger and more legible is the lettering of Mr. Rushmore, even though his line was necessarily crowded for the sake of *display.

The importance of dignified lettering in effecting the sale of drawings and designs

WAY·HOME

WAY-HOME

that require lettering, such as book and catalogue covers, title-pages, posters, book-plates, trade-marks, and advertisements, cannot be over-estimated.

The American designer has little use for any alphabets other than the " Roman " and modifications of the Roman, except in making advertisements. Pages 108 and 109 show this alphabet in its accepted classic form. The proportions of its letters and the selection of lines to be shaded or to be made thin are the outcome of centuries of experimentation and use. Other arrangements of the thick and the thin lines have been attempted but without improve-

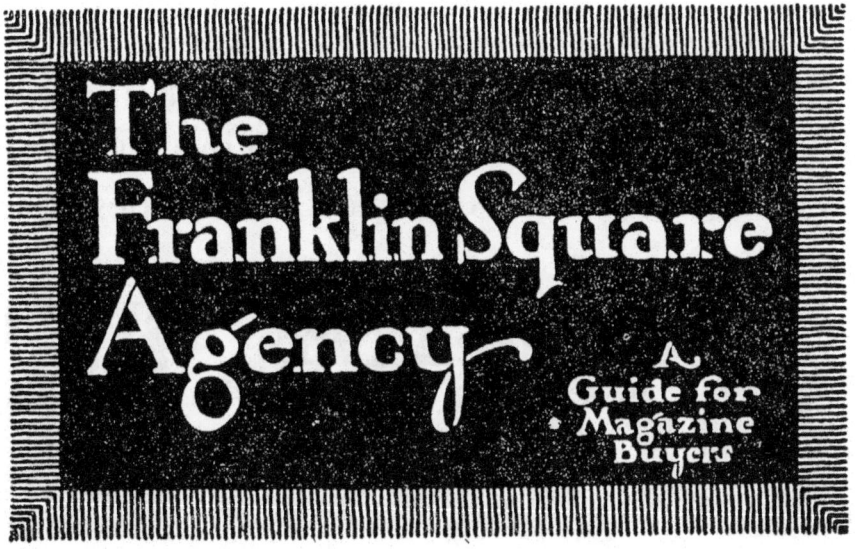

Eccentric lettering by Rushmore.

ment upon the so-called classic examples.

Perhaps the most striking thing about these letters is their "typical squareness of outline."

The manner in which the Latin scholars held their pens is supposed to be responsible for the arrangement of thick and thin lines. The up-stroke produced a thin line, and the down-stroke a thick or shaded line.

Brown gives us the following three rules based upon the use of the pen for the distribution of thin and thick lines:

(*a*) Never shade horizontal lines.

(*b*) Always accent the sloping, down-strokes that run from left to right, including the " swash " lines, or flying tails, of Q and R; but never shade those lines that

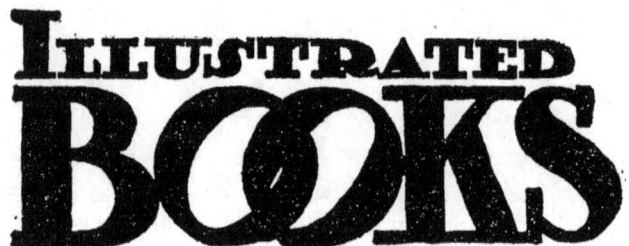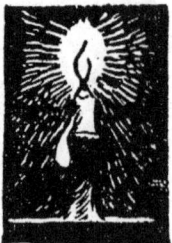

Heavy-face Roman letters.

slope up from left to right, with a single exception in the case of the letter Z.

(*c*) Always accent the directly vertical lines, except those of the N, which seem originally to have been made with an up-stroke of the pen, and the first line of the

M. On the round letters, the accents should be placed on the sides of the circle.

The little cross-stroke finishing the free ends of all lines of Roman capital letters is called the " serif." It gives uniformity and finish.

The middle horizontal lines of B, E, F, and H are commonly placed slightly above center, as are the junctions of K and X.

The making of the letter S gives much trouble to students. The difficulty will disappear if the letter be constructed upon the numeral 8, thus:

8SS

The upper section of the letters B, E, K, S, and Z should be less in breadth than the lower section.

Although our alphabet is very different from the hieroglyphics of the Egyptians, we are probably somewhat indebted to their character-writing.

A small portion of our alphabet dates from a few hundred years B.C.

The type in use by the printers of the present day has two forms, a larger and a smaller, which in the printing offices are called "upper case" and "lower case." The upper case are the capitals, his-

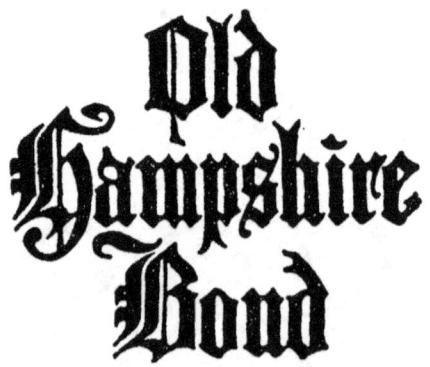

One example of "black letter."

torically termed the "majuscule." The lower case are the small letters, more properly the "minuscule." Manuscript writers adopted the second form (minuscule) because it can be more rapidly ex-

SOLDIERS ALL

PORTRAITS AND SKETCHES OF THE MEN OF THE A·E·F·

by

Joseph Cummings Chase

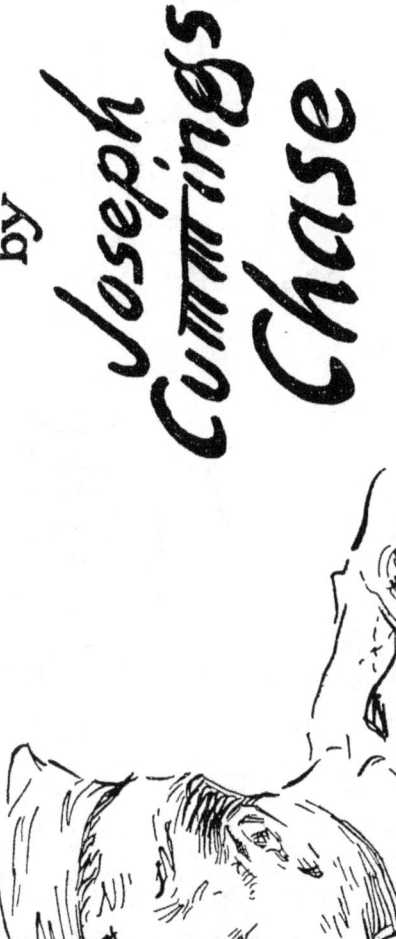

Example of Roman lettering used for a book cover.

ecuted and is more legible upon areas
where much lettering is employed.

It appears that Charlemagne (crowned
A.D. 800) did more than any one else to
perfect lettering and make it uniform.
Lewis F. Day in his " Alphabets Old and
New " tells us that it was through this
emperor's influence that the Church of

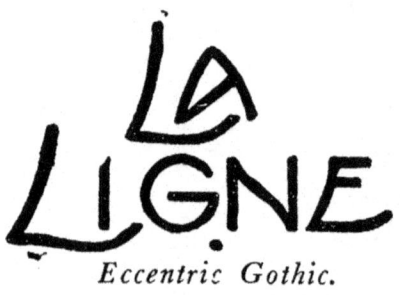

Eccentric Gothic.

Rome employed scribes capable of developing the art of lettering. From the pens
of these artists came the minuscule, or
small letters. Up to this time the capitals
only had been in use.

M, D, C, L, X, V, and I were generally
employed to express numbers previous to
the fifteenth century. It was then that
the " Arabic " numerals, so-called, were
introduced in Christian Europe. But ex-

cept for the numbers 1 and 9, and the cipher 0, none of the numerals which we use are truly Arabic.

Just why hand-lettering should be employed to-day where printers' type is so nearly mathematically perfect is not always understood.

The hand-letterer can so arrange the

Ce qu'on en pense

Eccentric Roman.

spacing of his letters as to make his lines more easy to read and more uniform in effect.

The unyielding letters of the type-foundry very frequently come together awkwardly.

Some of the best letterers, before "inking in" their letters, correct the penciled letters as to proportion and spacing with the lettering turned upside down.

SO-CALLED "GOTHIC" LETTERS

O Q C G S
I D P B R
U J &
L T F E H
N Z M K
V A W Y X
1 2 3 4 5 6 7 8 9 0

The student must become thoroughly accustomed to the proportions of the letters of the Roman alphabet.

Lettering must be (*a*) legible, (*b*) beautiful, and (*c*) dignified.

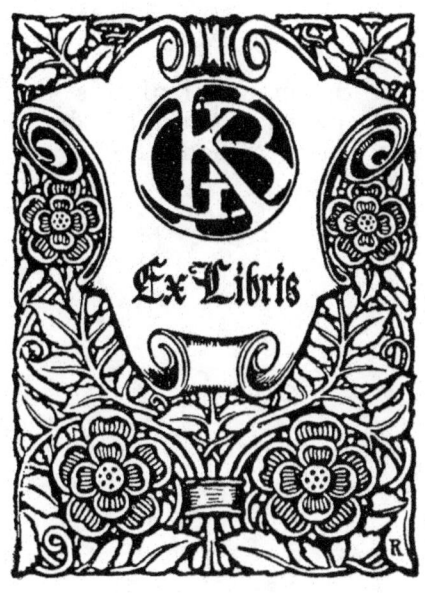

Book plate by Rushmore.

The " Old English " is a type of " black letter," but has gone out of use, except for infrequent decorative effects where legibility is not very important. See p. 116.

The unshaded alphabet shown on the previous page, having all its lines of equal thickness, is called " Modern Gothic." The term " Egyptian " is sometimes applied to it, although it resembles Egyptian hiero-glyphics in no point whatsoever.

Its proportions are those of the Roman. It might be called an unshaded Roman alphabet.

NOTE. Much of the material of this section on Lettering is taken from " Decorative Design " by the same author, published by John Wiley & Sons, Inc.

THE USE OF FLOWERS IN DESIGN

THE USE OF FLOWERS IN DESIGN

THERE is so much pleasure to be derived from the making of designs and there is so much profit as well, that no book on drawing would be complete without a chapter on this subject. The principles referred to in the chapter on Pictorial Composition are the same as those we must consider in this chapter,—Harmony, Dominance and Subordination, Balance and Symmetry, and the consideration of Tangential Junction. We are now concerned with surface enrichment by means of conventionalized ornament, particularly when these ornaments are forms conventionalized from nature. Natural

NOTE. Design here discussed is Decorative, or Applied—sometimes called Design of Two Dimensions.

forms should not be *copied* for design without exercising the power of invention. Literal imitation does not make successful decoration. The experienced designer has certain calculated ways of arriving at good motives suitable for the working out of any problem. He is able to adjust, to arrange, to modify, until his problem of surface-covering or space-filling is fittingly solved. This process in each problem involves a careful consideration and development of the peculiarities of shape and natural growth. In the course of this consideration and development, the designer, by simplifications and combinations, invents fresh and individual expressions of his art.

To utilize plant-growth and other natural forms properly for decorating given spaces or surfaces, it is necessary to employ a process called conventionalization. CONVENTIONALIZATION consists in keeping the general characteristics of a natural form, and omitting small details and accidents of growth, as the method of applying the design may require. It usually includes emphasis upon the geometric basis underlying natural forms. It is probable that conventionalization originated in the limitations imposed by the material used.

Conventionalization is of two kinds, (*a*) formal, and (*b*) informal. Broadly speaking, it is *formal* when purely decorative shapes and arrangements are devel-

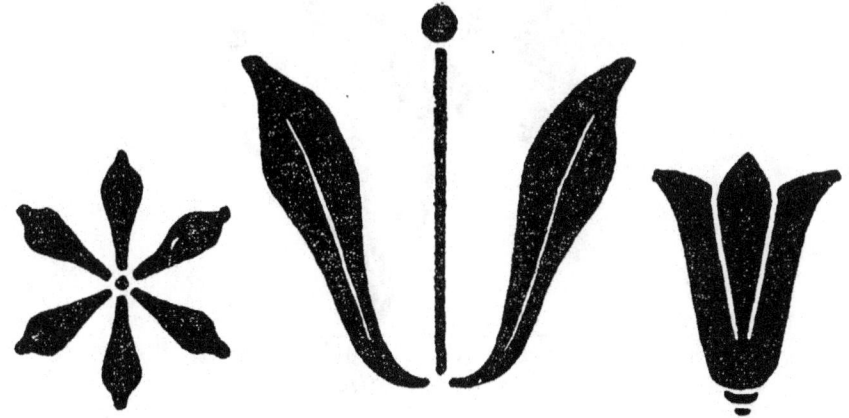

(a) *Three examples of formal conventionalization.*

oped *without* perspective appearance, even though natural form and growth be taken as a guide. It is *informal* when purely decorative shapes and arrangements are developed *with* perspective appearance.

It is called informal, even though small details are rejected.

The accompanying flower-plates from "Decorative Design," a text-book by the same author, show a series of steps by which the designer arrived at certain conventionalizations adapted to various uses

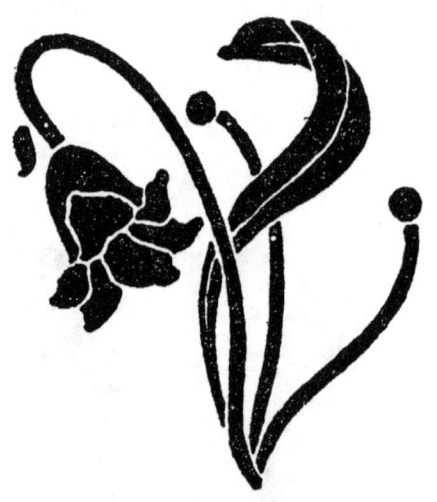

(b) *An example of informal conventionalization.*

in decorative design. Detailed drawings made from living plants and flowers are especially valuable as a source of design motives, but it is not always possible for the student, or even for the professional designer, to get these. Photographs from books of reference pertaining to plant and flower growth, insect and animal life, will be found very helpful. The photographs used as the basis of steps in the accompanying flower - plates were selected from easily obtained flower and seed catalogues.

The *first step* (see page 132) is merely an outline drawing made from the photograph. The tendency in making an outline sketch is to strive for an " artistic " effect, which usually results in a fuzzy roughness. Such a sketch is of no help at all to the designer. He must have a carefully considered outline of each of the many shapes contained in the photograph of flower, leaf, and stem. To insure such a consideration by the student, it is well, in the developing of conventionalized motives from flowers, to separate each particle or segment from the others. The outline will then resemble a stencil, because of the little " canals " which surround each shape and separate it from the others.

When these canals are used, they should be kept of consistent width.

In the *second step* (see page 132), it is then possible to make a really artistic arrangement by selecting from the first step the most attractive segments, simplifying, adjusting, combining, but always preserving the *type* of the flower, leaf, and stem. The second step, then, is not necessarily a conventionalization; but it must be an ornament as artistic as the student is capable of producing.

The *third step* (see page 133) is an invention — a bilateral or " twin " unit. These units are used in " all-over " patterns for unlimited areas, such as wall papers, and upholstery, and other textiles. This third step *is* necessarily a conventionalization. The fact that such a unit will be repeated many times in the pattern requires that the unit be simple and well contained within itself, otherwise it will look sprawling and uncontrolled.

As suggested in the chapter on Pictorial

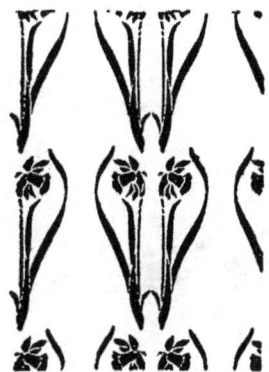

(a) Units placed in vertical rows.

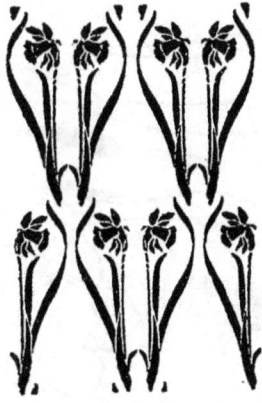

(b) Units placed in horizontal rows.

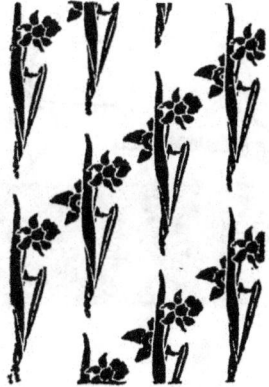

(c) Units placed in oblique rows.

Composition, the contour of background spaces contained within the unit, and of background spaces formed by the juxtaposition of the units in the "repeat," is as important as the shapes of the units themselves. The importance of the foregoing sentence cannot be exaggerated.

Every part of the motive should be clean-cut and firm. The use of the canals is by no means essential to the production of a decorative motive, but it will be found helpful, particularly in elementary work. If a stencil is to be made for transferring the unit, the canals have allowed for the stencil cutting. Or if a poster outline is

Second
Step

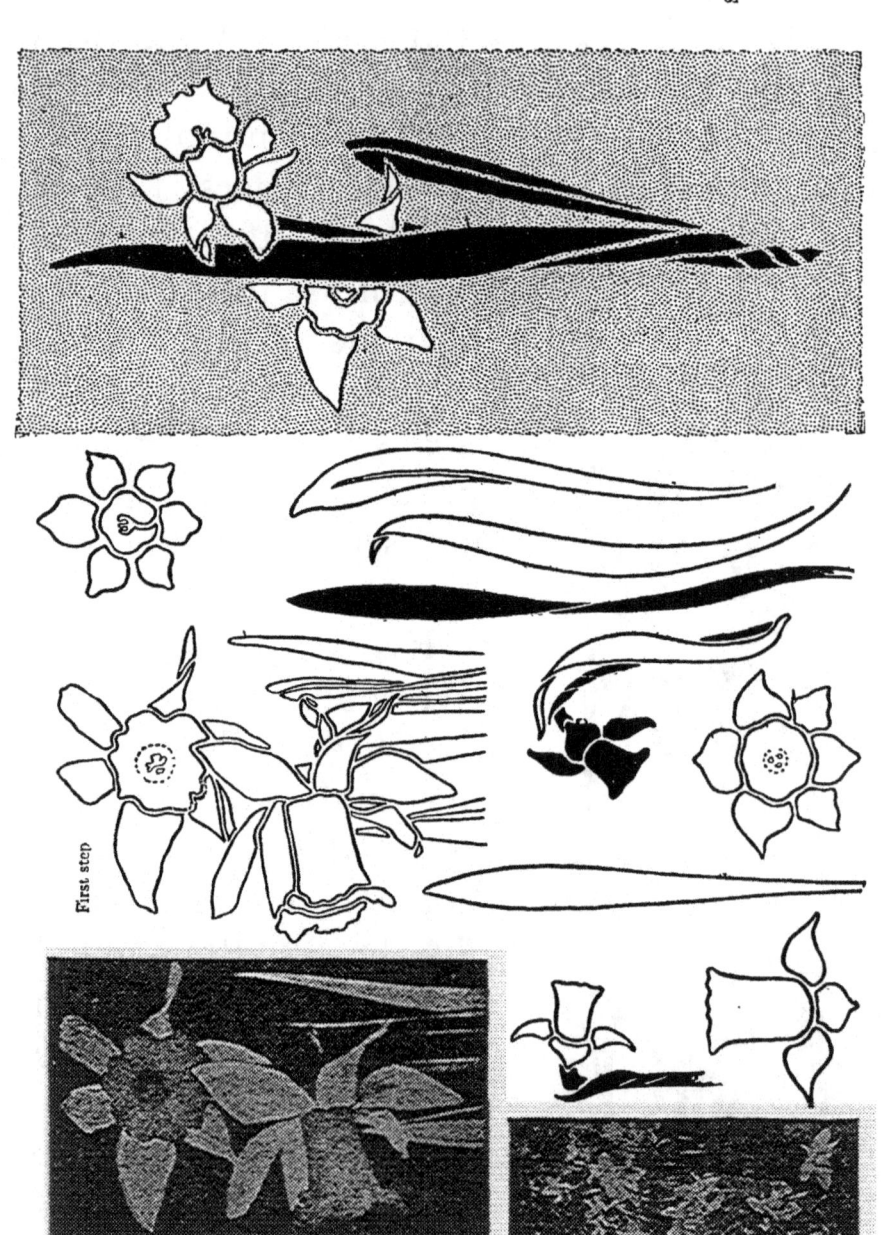

First step

First step: Making a careful outline drawing.
Second step: Creating an informal ornament with shapes selected from the first step.

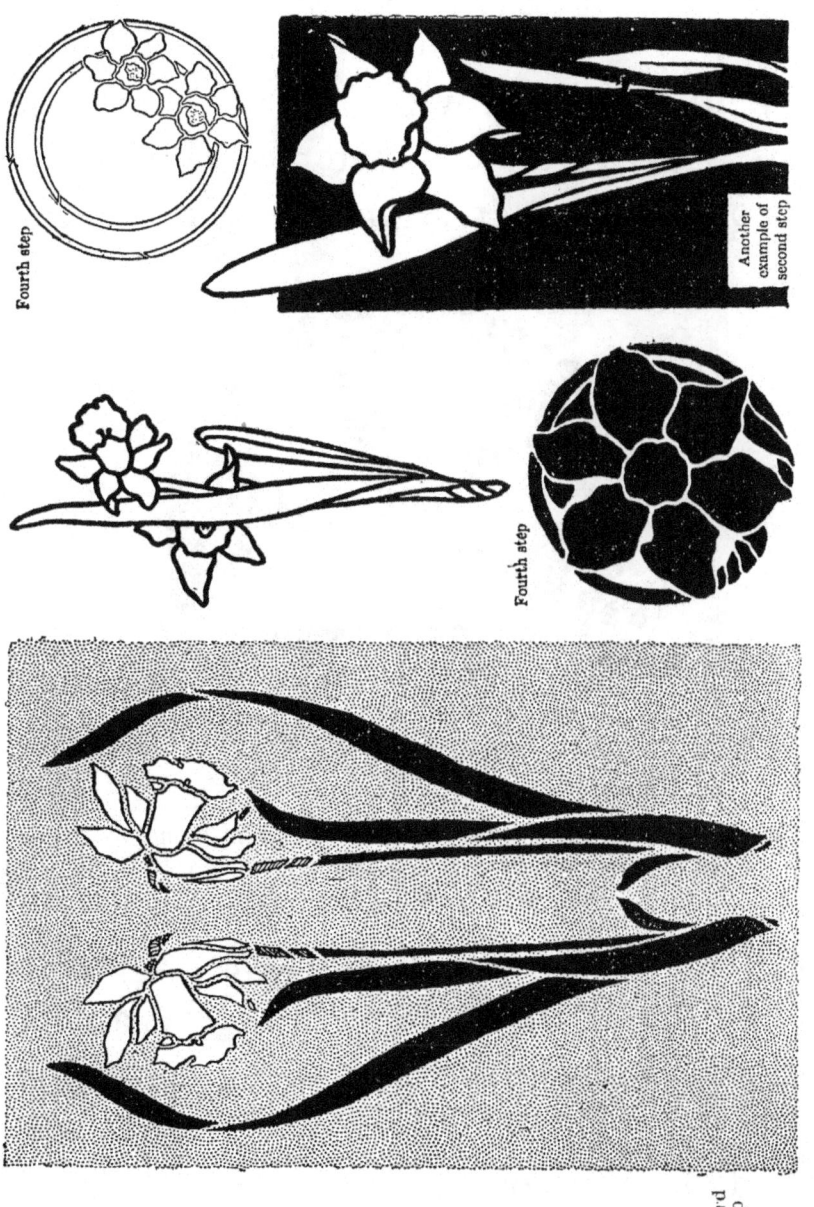

Fourth step

Another example of second step

Fourth step

Third step

Third step: Making a bilateral or "twin" unit for an all-over pattern (see next page). Fourth step: Space-filling.

111

to be used, as in so many examples from the Japanese, the canals are exactly in the position of the intended outline and need only to be filled with the outline color. This will avert the disaster of obliterating any of the smaller segments of the design

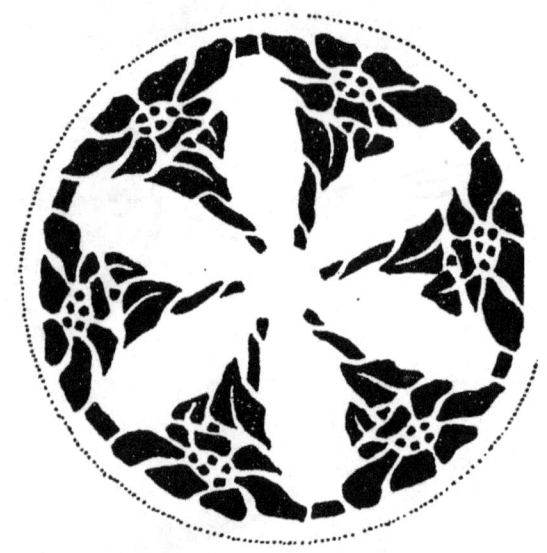

Design for table-mat, showing the im-
portance of the contour of back-
ground spaces.

by the overlapping of the heavy outlines.

The *fourth step* (see page 133) is a decoration for any given area — circle, ellipse, oval, heart shape, rectangle, triangle, diamond, kite shape, or vase form. This is called space-filling. Under this head come title-pages, heading and tail-pieces, initial letters, trade-marks, book plates, some kinds of book covers, book-rack ends, borders, table mats, titles, china decoration. The competent designer must have the ability to decorate any given space-shape

Design showing the importance of the contour of the background space.

with properly balanced or symmetrical design. Backgrounds may, of course, be treated in many ways other than by plain tones of black, or white, or color. Backgrounds may be enriched by lines or spots, light upon dark, or dark upon light.

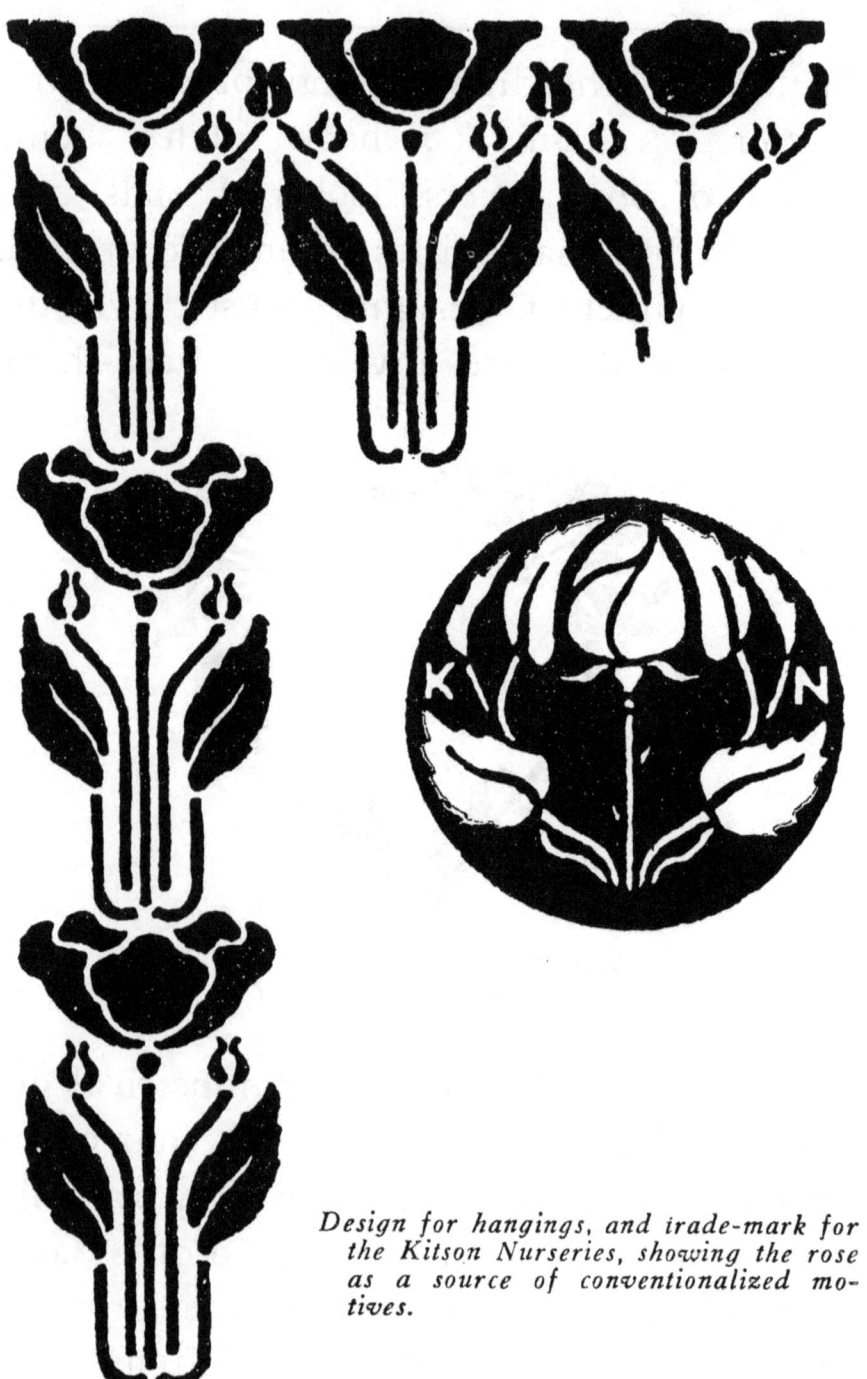

Design for hangings, and trade-mark for the Kitson Nurseries, showing the rose as a source of conventionalized motives.

PHOTO-ENGRAVING

PHOTO-ENGRAVING

SINCE drawings must so often be made with a view to their being reproduced by photo-engraving, the necessity for the draughtsman to understand the process of the making of " cuts " is apparent. The term " photo-engraving " indicates the process by which from the original drawing a " cut," that is, an engraved plate, is made for printing photographic reproductions of that drawing. There are different kinds of photo-engraving because of the demands of reproducing drawings made with different mediums upon different surfaces. These different kinds vary widely in cost. Lithography and hand-engraving are not included in so-called photo-engraving. Photo-engraving consists of line-cuts and half-tones and combinations of the two. Line-cuts cost ten or fifteen cents per square inch. Half-tones cost twenty cents, or more, per square inch. Combinations of half-tones and line-cuts can be made costing the price per square inch of half-tones plus the price per inch for line-cuts. A duograph consists of two half-tone plates for printing any two colors. It costs about fifty cents per square inch. Reproductions for printing three colors with three half-tone plates — usually printed in red, yellow, and blue — cost about $1.25 per square inch.

Line-cut photo-engravings are made as follows: The drawing is placed in front of a camera and photographed. The size of reproduction is determined by the distance to which the camera is removed from the drawing and by the focus of the lens. The photographer determines the desired distance by means of the ground glass " finder " of the camera, upon which are linear measurements, horizontal, and vertical. A negative is developed, the film is stripped from the camera-plate, and placed reversed upon plate glass which is then locked in a frame against a zinc or copper plate to insure close contact. The surface of this zinc or copper is sensitized after the manner of a camera-plate. This is exposed to the rays of a powerful light which acts upon the metal surface through the film-negative, making a faint etching of the picture upon the metal. This etching is developed by the use of acids which act upon the surface of the metal and thus develop the delicate etching into a deeper one. Whatever parts of the metal were covered by the blacks of the film-negative are by the acid eaten away and the parts that were covered by the whites of the negative are left unaffected. These unaffected parts are the ones that receive the ink and show in the printing. After the metal plate has been mounted upon a thickness of wood to make it the height of

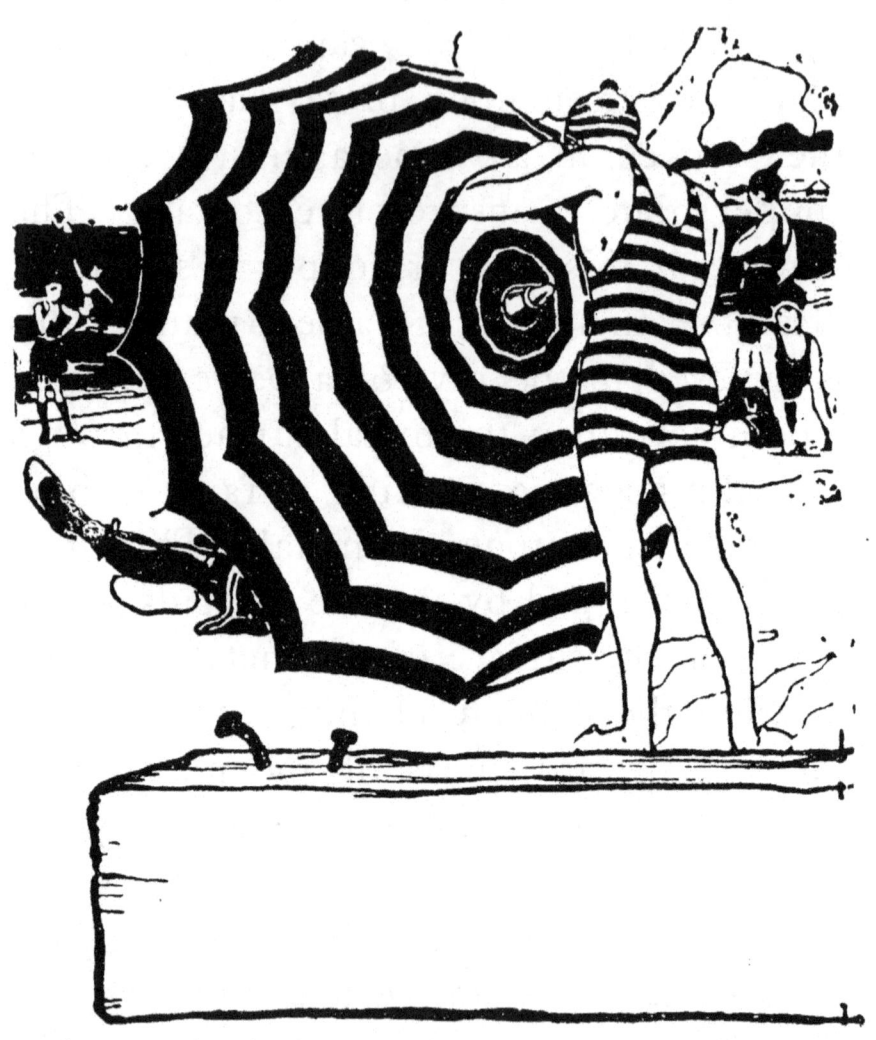

An example of a so-called line-cut, or "zinc etching." See other examples on pages 37 and 75.

type it is ready for the printer. These line-cuts do not reproduce any intermediate tones between black and white, therefore drawings to be reproduced by this process must be made of black and white only. Any part of the drawing which is not black and white, which reproduces at all, will print black. Drawings for reproduction should be made somewhat larger than the dimensions of the intended reproduction — from one-third greater to four times greater. If a drawing is made twice the size of the intended reproduction the lines of that drawing will not only be one-half as long as those of the corresponding lines of the original, but will also be one-half as thick, consequently the lines of the original drawing should be made of a thickness sufficient to permit of this reduction.

This is the cheapest of the photo-engraving processes. It is the best adapted for printing upon coarse paper. Its being the cheapest does not indicate that it is the

least attractive, for black and white drawings have a quality all their own.

There are manufactured mechanical
stencil patterns by the use of which tone
effects may be given to the surface of line-
cuts. The best of these are called by the
name of their inventor, Ben Day. The
draughtsman does not attempt to apply
these stencils to his original drawing, but
indicates by number upon his drawing the
particular Ben Day tone that he wishes applied to a certain surface area of the reproduction. The engraver can follow the directions indicated, and apply that particular stencil pattern to the section indicated.
This application is made to the surface
of the metal itself, before the acid etching.
The draughtsman should indicate upon his
drawing his directions to the engraver with
a blue pencil, because blue is the color
which does not reproduce in the photographing of a line-cut, therefore blue

NOTE. Background of second step on page 132 shows a
Ben Day tone.

markings will not interfere with the reproduction of the drawing.

Half-tone reproduction is in many ways identical with that of line-cuts. It is different in that in the camera when photographing the drawing, there are placed two " screens," one with a ruling of horizontal lines, the other with a ruling of vertical lines, so that the two together form tiny squares by the crossing of their lines. The photograph upon the film, as a result, is divided into tiny squares, because the tiny squares are photographed together with the drawing. The surface of the metal is etched with acids, as in the case of line-cuts. The tiny squares produced on the film, and therefrom upon the metal, are variously affected by the acid, some being etched away more completely than others, the difference depending upon the amount of light that penetrated the film at each individual square. In printing,

NOTE. See pages 73 and 77 for examples of half-tone reproduction.

squares that are least etched away receive the most ink and therefore print the darkest. The " screens," as they are called, are of different degrees of fineness, ranging from sixty lines per lineal inch to two hundred. The finer screens are intended for cuts to be printed upon smooth coated papers, while the coarser screens are intended for coarser paper and are better adapted to the quick drying ink used by newspapers. In the coarser screens the little squares are plainly visible, whereas the finer screens reproduce more perfectly the delicacy of detail of the original drawing.

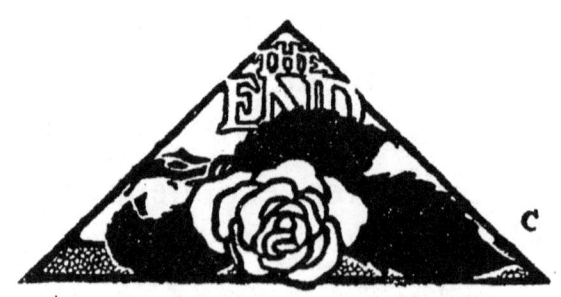

A " line-cut." see page 143.

www.ingramcontent.com/pod-product-compliance
Lightning Source LLC
Chambersburg PA
CBHW051217170526
45166CB00005B/1931